T0339729

Cambridge Elements ≡

Elements in Ethics
edited by
Ben Eggleston
University of Kansas
Dale E. Miller
Old Dominion University, Virginia

ETHICAL CONSTRUCTIVISM

Carla Bagnoli
University of Modena and Reggio Emilia

CAMBRIDGE
UNIVERSITY PRESS

CAMBRIDGE
UNIVERSITY PRESS

University Printing House, Cambridge CB2 8BS, United Kingdom

One Liberty Plaza, 20th Floor, New York, NY 10006, USA

477 Williamstown Road, Port Melbourne, VIC 3207, Australia

314–321, 3rd Floor, Plot 3, Splendor Forum, Jasola District Centre,
New Delhi – 110025, India

103 Penang Road, #05–06/07, Visioncrest Commercial, Singapore 238467

Cambridge University Press is part of the University of Cambridge.

It furthers the University's mission by disseminating knowledge in the pursuit of
education, learning, and research at the highest international levels of excellence.

www.cambridge.org
Information on this title: www.cambridge.org/9781108706605
DOI: 10.1017/9781108588188

First published 2022

A catalogue record for this publication is available from the British Library.

ISBN 978-1-108-70660-5 Paperback
ISSN 2516-4031 (online)
ISSN 2516-4023 (print)

Ethical Constructivism

Elements in Ethics

DOI: 10.1017/9781108588188
First published online: January 2022

Carla Bagnoli
University of Modena and Reggio Emilia

Author for correspondence: Carla Bagnoli, carla.bagnoli@gmail.com

Abstract: Ethical constructivism holds that truths about the relation between rationality, morality, and agency are best understood as constructed by correct reasoning, rather than discovered or invented. Unlike other metaphors used in metaethics, construction brings to light the generative and dynamic dimension of practical reason. On the resultant picture, practical reasoning is not only productive but also self-transforming and socially empowering. The main task of this Element is to illustrate how constructivism has substantially modified and expanded the agenda of metaethics by refocusing on rational agency and its constitutive principles. In particular, this Element identifies, compares, and discusses the prospects and failures of the main strands of constructivism regarding the powers of reason in responding to the challenges of contingency. While Kantian, Humean, Aristotelian, and Hegelian theories sharply differ in their constructivist strategies, they provide compelling accounts of the rational articulation required for an inclusive and unified ethical community.

Keywords: ethics, rationality, agency, morality, Kant

ISBNs: 9781108706605 (PB), 9781108588188 (OC)
ISSNs: 2516-4031 (online), 2516-4023 (print)

Contents

Introduction

Moral obligations seem to make claims that are both objective and universally binding. However, do we have any reasons to abide by morality? If we do, are such reasons grounded in our culture or in our nature as human beings, or do they otherwise derive from rationality itself? In the first case, reasons apply authoritatively only to a given group or community at a given time. In the second case, moral reasons bind us in a broad but contingent manner. In the third case, a strong argument can be made that by rooting reasons for moral action in rationality, one vindicates moral claims that are both universal and authoritative. This is an appealing prospect only insofar as rationality itself binds us all with normative authority and offers us normative reasons for action.

These issues have been central to philosophical reflection at least since Socrates. A prominent approach in recent debates asserts that normative truths about the relation between rationality, morality, and agency are best captured by developing the metaphor of *construction*. The general idea is that truths about our reasoned actions as rational and moral agents are the constructs of correct practical reasoning, rather than those produced by conventions, grasped via insight, or otherwise discovered or learned through practice. Importantly, there is a method to construction, although its status and features have been envisioned differently by various constructivist theories. As a result, explaining what unifies such views and what distinguishes them from others has proven to be a challenging task.

The varieties of constructivist theories all involve different agendas and scopes. The most ambitious of these theories purport to provide insights that prove to be disruptive of the way in which ethical theorizing itself is partitioned and understood in the debates of the first half of the twentieth century. As initially conceived by John Rawls, the constructivist project aims to uncover theoretical resources that can address crucial philosophical questions about ethical objectivity and the place of morality in human life. To this end, Rawls revisits Kant's conception of "practical reason," a notion that has long been discounted in analytic ethics due to its metaphysical commitments (Allison 2006; O'Shea 2006). Rawls believes that the main features of Kant's conception of practical reason can be preserved while minimizing the metaphysical implications, adopting the metaphor of construction to illustrate the very activity of reason, which is governed by a formal norm: the requirement of universality. The Kantian promise is that by appealing to such a norm about how to reason, rational agents can agree on what action to take, although they may be driven by diverse interests and concerned with contrasting conceptions of what constitutes the good life. In its most ambitious formulation, the universality serves not only as the constitutive norm of practical reasoning but also as the norm of self-constitution for rational agents.

The Kantian project has been modulated and continued in various ways that substantially depart from Kant's own notion of practical reason. Most contemporary constructivists adhere to a minimalistic understanding of the nature and powers of practical reason, although not all of them deny a naturalistic moral ontology and some even engage in a cautious and critical strain of metaphysics. Some varieties of constructivism build upon the critique of Kantian constructivism and leave behind its most distinctive aspiration, that is, the vindication of the objectivity and universal authority of moral obligations by way of the features of rational agency. Others develop the Kantian insights in different directions, refocusing the agenda on the dynamics of social interactions.

To account for constructivism as a distinctive cluster of theories, in this essay, I give serious credence to the notion of "construction" as a label for a distinctive mode of rational justification that also captures the authoritative nature of normative truths. Construction names the correct form of practical reasoning that *constitutes* and explains normative truths, principles, and values. Thus understood, the metaphor of construction is not a mere heuristic; it carries a distinct explanatory force.

This approach promises a more perspicuous definition of constructivism, which accommodates the various strains of constructivism and explains what unifies them by focusing on three nodal elements: its agents, method, and target domain. The varieties of constructivism will be distinguished by specifying the nodes of the construction. By identifying their distinctive features, we will be better poised to assess their merits. We will pay particular attention to their capacity to address the problems that they are designed to answer, as well as the resources available to respond to the challenges posed by their opponents. However, the main task of this Element is to illustrate how constructivism has contributed to reformulating the central problems in metaethics regarding the nature of normative and moral reasons. Instead of moral constructivism, this essay will focus on constructivist theories about practical reason, with special attention to moral norms. Despite the formidable challenges that such theories face, they have substantially modified and expanded the agenda of metaethics to include issues on the normative dimensions of reasoning and moral authority, which are not yet fully explored. The scope of inquiry is limited in two ways. First, the Element does not have the ambition to address all constructivist theories advanced in the history of philosophy; thus, there are many worthwhile theories that are left out. Second, within the narrow debate under consideration, the focus is on metaethical issues rather than on constructivist methods, which provide guidance in first-order moral theorizing. In particular, I have organized the debate around the constructivist attempts to defend ethical objectivity against the challenges posited by contingency.

The roadmap to this Element is as follows. Section 1 introduces an account of John Rawls' expectations regarding the promise of Kant's philosophical method as a new entry point into a stale debate about objectivity, which is divided between two metaethical positions: skepticism and realism. For Kant, the norms of reason are a priori and necessary, and their constructive activity generates and grounds moral obligations, which are *practical necessities*, categorically and universally binding for all rational beings. This theory has inspired contemporary debates regarding the source of normative authority and the type of necessity involved in moral discourse.

Section 2 focuses on Christine Korsgaard's theory, which argues for the authority of moral obligations by rendering them *inescapable* insofar as they spring from our identity as agents. Not only does this powerful theory build on Kant's insights, but it also aims to remedy some of the alleged shortcomings of Kant's ethics by refraining from metaphysics and accommodating the contingency of our social identities. Yet the argument aims to establish an inescapable relation between the constitutive norms of rationality and morality. But is a commitment to rational agency inescapable?

Section 3 addresses the issue of the *contingency* of moral and rational standards, which features prominently in Humean constructivism. Building on the critique of Kantian transcendental arguments, Sharon Street defends the formality of the practical standpoint and its commitment to a measure of relativism. Nonetheless, by appealing to human nature, Humean constructivism can explain a general – albeit contingent – agreement on a common core of moral principles. Is human nature a robust enough concept to ground such an agreement?

Section 4 addresses theories that emphasize the concrete social dynamics of rational deliberation. Aristotelian constructivism treats practical reason as incomplete and refocuses on practical wisdom as the *concrete* exemplar of its social completion. Other theories privilege the practices of mutual recognition and appropriate the Hegelian approach to ethics, arguing that practical reason manifests itself in historical social forms. The claim about the historicity of practical reason requires a "metaphysics of *actuality*" or else it falls back to relativism. This approach raises the challenge of the intended scope of practical reason: What are the bounds of the moral community, and how can they be rationally negotiated?

Section 5 takes stock of the preceding discussion about how constructivism makes progress on some traditional issues in metaethics and points toward promising new directions of research that exploit the metaphor of construction even further, in service of an expanding moral community.

1 Objectivity as a Practical Task

Ethical constructivism, with its ancient roots, is generally understood to be a theory that denies the objectivity of values and morals by insisting that they are man-made, i.e., akin to artifacts rather than parts of the fabric of the world.[1] Faced with Euthyphro's dilemma on whether values are true because they are recognized to be good or they are recognized as good because they are true, constructivists typically side with the former assertion. By contrast, in his *Dewey Lectures* on Kantian constructivism in moral theory, John Rawls elaborates on ethical constructivism as an objectivist account of ethics. Ethical objectivity has been understood in various ways, but primarily, it has been understood to entail that ethical properties are mind-independent and hence require a robust form of realism. By contrast, Rawls proposes an account of ethical objectivity, which is rival to robust realism.[2] The term "constructive" does not entail that values or moral facts are subjective or relative, but rather that their objectivity is of practical significance to human beings. Rawls retrieves Kant's moral theory as a distinctive model of ethical theorizing whose absence has hindered the progress of moral and political theory (Rawls 1980). Since this judgment undoubtedly depends on Rawls' assessment of the state of the play, this section begins with an account of his expectations regarding the methods of ethical theory.

1.1 Ethical Methods and the Standards of Objectivity

Rawls' interest in Kant's philosophy is best appreciated against the backdrop of the metaethical debate of the twentieth century.[3] Rawls turns to Kant's moral theory in an attempt to advance the issue of ethical objectivity by rescuing it from the quagmire that is the debate surrounding the ontological nature of values and moral truths. According to the mainstream view, ethical objectivity is a metaethical problem to be solved by investigating the logical and semantic

---

[1] Cf. O'Neill 1989, p. 1. Some pre-Kantian views, such as that of Spinoza and Hume, could be regarded as varieties of constructivism that attempt to account for a sort of objectivity, though not in the sense I am about to specify.

[2] As the debate developed, many others defended accounts of ethical objectivity that reject mind-independence and thus the commitment to robust forms of moral realism, (see, e.g., Gibbard 1990; McDowell 1995; Wong 2008; James 2012.

[3] Kant's rediscovery has motivated a similar agenda regarding normativity within the philosophy of mind, see McDowell 1981; Putnam 1981.

properties of moral language. The underlying assumption is that metaethics, understood as the semantic analysis of ethical concepts and judgments, is neutral and independent with regard to any normative and substantive issues. Contrary to this view, Rawls argues that metaethical inquiry stands on normative grounds and that any progress in metaethics depends on and results from progress in moral theory (Rawls 1951, pp. 286–302).

While realists and antirealists have discussed the ontological credentials of the judgments that aspire toward objectivity,[4] Rawls underscores the various criteria of objectivity and reconceptualizes ethical objectivity as a *practical* problem.[5] By considering the criterion of objectivity that aptly serves as a practical task, Rawls parts ways with moral realists and antirealists alike: they share a *representationalist* view of judgments, according to which their main function is to represent a domain of objects.[6]

Uninterested in the ontological pursuit, Rawls aims to vindicate the objectivity of moral knowledge by setting aside the current options internal to the realism versus antirealism debate and refocusing on the methods:

> [T]he objectivity or subjectivity of moral knowledge turns not on the question whether ideal value entities exist or whether moral judgements are caused by emotions or whether there is a variety of moral codes the world over, but simply on the question: does there exist a reasonable method for validating or invalidating given or proposed moral rules and those decisions made on the basis of them? (Rawls 1951, p. 177).

1.2 Kant's Constructivism

According to Kant, objective practical knowledge is the achievement of practical reason. The activity of reason is governed by norms of practical reasoning, and Rawls understands these claims as commitments to constructivism. The metaphor of construction is borrowed not only from geometry but also from the building trade (Ak A 738–39/B 766–67, A 711/B 739), and Kantian constructivists deploy the latter to illustrate the activity and progress of reason.[7]

---

[4] Realists conceive of it in terms of ontology, and antirealists in terms of practical inference and psychological mechanisms such as the projection of sentiments or social processes of reification.

[5] This move may be thought to be akin to those invoked by expressivists, see, e.g., Blackburn 1988; Lenman 1998. However, the notion of construction at play in Kantian constructivism is distinctive and should not be assimilated to the kind of projection of sentiments at works in quasi-realism. I shall be back to this issue in Section 3.6.

[6] From a semantic point of view, representationalism is the root of the divide between realism and antirealism, see Putnam 1990, pp. 20, 23; Rorty 1991, pp. 445, 448.

[7] Ethical constructivists privilege the metaphor from the building trade, see Rawls 1993; O'Neill 2015, pp. 25–37.

1.2.1 Constructions of Reason

The metaphor of construction proves useful in explicating the powers of reason as well as its activity.[8] Claims of reason are established not by appealing to particular facts of the matter but by uncovering the guiding norms of the activity of reason itself. The term "construction" names a distinctive form of rational justification that preserves the autonomy of reason and shows that the law is inherent in the very idea of rational agency. The constructivist conception of practical reason is inconsistent with the realist claim that there is an order of value prior to and independent of the autonomous activity of reason itself. Consequently, practical reasoning does not consist in tracking down moral facts or recognizing any external sources of value. Rather, it is a form of self-government.

1.2.2 The Nodes of Construction

To characterize the activity of reason, it is useful to focus on three nodes: (i) the target domain, (ii) the profile of relevant agents, and (iii) the method of rational justification. This matrix allows us to distinguish between the varieties of constructivism according to their respective conception of each node and the relevant relations between these nodes.

Kant's moral theory constructs the content of the moral doctrine, that is, the *totality of the imperatives for what one ought to do.* Ordinary agents possess a rough and ready understanding of their moral duties. Philosophical inquiry improves this basic understanding by rendering the grounds of moral obligation coherent and transparent. This improvement provides a variety of self-knowledge, that is, knowledge of oneself as a "practical subject," capable of reasoning and acting under the ideal and constraints of practical norms, including the moral law. This is because pure practical philosophy involves something like practical reason's knowledge of itself.

The second node specifies the type of agents who can take an interest in action – that is, act on principles – without being driven by prior motives. The specification of the profile of these agents pertains to "moral psychology," which is understood as the study of the role played by a conception of the person, in moral thinking as well as in the governance of personal moral relations (Herman 2000, p. xii). Unlike other models of rational action, Kantian constructivism explicitly builds upon a distinctive account of rational agency, which is assumed to be implicit in ordinary moral and prudential thinking. Within such an account, people represent themselves and others *as*

---

[8] Rawls 1980, 1989, 2000; Kant G 4: 441–44; C2 5: 35–41, 153, 157.

free and equal. These features of the profile of rational agents play a recognizably key role in the activity of rational justification. Ultimately, this profile sets the stage against which the problem of rational action arises. Insofar as this profile invokes values such as freedom and equality, it is *rich*. In another sense, however, it is *minimal* because these features belong within the agent's self-representation and play a regulative role, although it is a debated issue what kind of metaphysics is entailed by this claim. Finally, the moral powers that rational agents attribute to themselves and others in ordinary moral thinking suffice to explain their interest in engaging in moral reasoning. To define rational construction, Rawls maintains that we need to identify the agents for whom the problem of rational justification arises. In short, the relevant agents are concerned with themselves and others as beings acting on reasons and capable of self-reflection but also entitled to demand reasons from others and required to support their claims on rational grounds.

This profile of the relevant agents aligns with the method of construction, which is designed to express the personality of rational agents. Any method expected to fulfill this function should respect the freedom and equality of persons. For Kant, the only method of thinking and acting that meets these requisites is the method of rational justification: this is the third node of construction. This is the *categorical imperative* (henceforth CI), which is also the supreme principle of morality.[9] Since this method is designed to reflect and conform to the moral experience of ordinary agents in their relations to one another, it is not itself constructed:

> The idea here is that not everything can be built. Every construction has a base, certain materials from which, as it were, to start. Although it is not, as we have seen above, constructed, but only exposed, the procedure of the imperative has a basis: the conception of free and equal persons as reasonable and rational, a conception that this procedure reflects (Rawls 2000, p. 258).[10]

The purported relation between the form of rational justification and the profile of rational agents is crucial in explaining how moral obligation binds human agents: although they are imperfect and limited in many ways, they are not restricted to instrumental reasoning. Unlike algorithms and other kinds of procedures, the CI ensures not only the objectivity of its outcomes but also its authority. By engaging in practical reasoning, we end up with "practical cognitions": normative truths that are applicable to all rational beings as well as

---

[9] The CI names the form of practical reasoning and the supreme principle of morality; instead, categorical imperatives refer to principles of rational actions that have passed the CI test and qualify as moral principles.

[10] This way of thinking of Kant's constructivism can be interestingly compared with Kant's hylomorphism, Engstrom 2009; Pollok 2017; Tenenbaum 2019; Schafer 2019a.

universally binding. Practical cognitions are requirements of reason and include moral obligations such as "respect others", and prudential obligations such as "Do not be inefficient". This is to say that their content is established and exacted by reason itself, not by human convention, persuasion, or force.

However, are rational requirements *really* binding? Are there normative reasons to act upon them? These questions arise for agents who regard themselves as capable of thinking and acting on principles. Moral principles are authoritative as rational requirements because the method of reasoning is extracted from the relevant conception of the person: "The conception of free and equal persons as reasonable and rational is the basis of the construction: if this conception and the powers of the moral personality – our humanity – did not come to life, so to speak, in human beings, the moral law would have no basis in the world" (Rawls 2000, p. 259). Moral obligations are binding because their contents are internally related to some features of rational agency. The practical efficacy of moral cognition is a crucial aspect of its objectivity, for if moral obligations did not bind human agents, then their objectivity would be merely chimerical.

For Rawls, Kant's critical method represents a theoretical option that is neglected if the metaethical map is organized around the centrality of the ontological question. More importantly, it promises to overcome the impasse of those metaethics, which consider action-guidingness and objectivity as forces pulling in opposite directions (Mackie 1977; Smith 1994). The constructivist conception of practical reason is defended as an alternative to both the realist construal of objectivity and the antirealist construal of action-guidingness.

1.2.3 Heteronomy as Moral Skepticism

According to Kant, reason is the source of all moral and epistemic authority; its authority is not derivative, and its domain extends to all rational agents. Kant's argument for this claim is largely negative (Kant G 4.441–44, 153, 157; C2 5.35–41). In his view, all previous ethical theories fail to vindicate the autonomy of reason due to heteronomy, which they are thus guilty of. All these theories conceive of moral authority as derived from and dependent on a source external to reason, such as nature, God, or social power. Any such authority, however, is conditional and can be questioned by reason. Ultimately, heteronomous theories cannot establish and vindicate the distinction between right and wrong. In short, skepticism toward the practical power of reason leads to moral skepticism about right and wrong. This argument targets sentimentalism and dogmatic rationalism.

By identifying sentiment as the origin of moral distinctions, Hume's senti-mentalism ascribes a solely instrumental role to reason (Kant G 4.441). The task of reason is to identify the appropriate means of achieving the ends offered by nature. The driving force of instrumental reason depends upon the occurrence of desire. As a consequence, sentimentalism provides a instrumental justification for moral obligation. Since the authority of moral obligation is derivative, it can only be conditional on the satisfaction of its antecedent; hence, it is unable to produce a universal agreement.[11]

The case against rationalism is not as straightforward as the one against sentimentalism,[12] and it addresses theories such as that of Christian Wolff and Gottfried Wilhelm Leibniz according to which the function of reason is to recognize and respond to reasons (Kant G 4.441–44; C2 5.41). By extension, the task of reasoning is to track an objective order of values that exist prior to and independently of reasoning. This indicates that this variety of rationalism is a heteronomous doctrine. But it may stand a better chance of establishing the authority of moral judgments because it can explain the efficacy of moral truths by noting that rational agents are expected to have a desire to act upon reason. However, the availability of this reply on behalf of rationalism does not prove that Kant's objection against heteronomy is successfully addressed only to the sentimentalist. Heteronomy is an error regarding the function of reason and its domain. If reason simply adapts to its object and thus reproduces ends beyond itself, then the practical function of reason is not affirmed. Its authority is conditional rather than categorical, and practical reasoning is instrumental in achieving the given ends. The autonomy of reason must be understood in an ontological sense: (practical) reason produces its objects, and it is authoritative with regard to the objects that it produces. It is precisely the thesis that the ends depend ontologically on the practical reason that distinguishes the practical use of reason from its theoretical function (Engstrom 2009, p. 119). More import-antly, the "existential dependence" of ends on reason explains their authority, since practical reason is nothing but rational will.[13]

---

[11] One may reply that the instrumentalist conception of practical rationality, while conditioned on human psychology, is sufficient to guarantee an agreement broad enough to ensure societal stability. This is the route taken by contemporary Humean constructivists, as we shall see in Section 3; though, it can be questioned that it is the view attributed to Hume himself.

[12] Rawls appreciates the weakness of the argument against rationalism, see Rawls 2000, pp. 253–54; cf. Stern 2012 for the argument that realism is not Kant's intended target.

[13] This statement may sound surprising since Rawls' slogan is that constructivism vindicates objectivity without ontology but recall that Rawls' target is robust moral realism. Furthermore, while Kant is the source of inspiration for Kantian constructivism, it is unlikely that he shares their anti-metaphysical approach; the point of Kant's constructivism is to ground practical reason in critical rather than dogmatic philosophy.

To wit, Kant's constructivism is an improvement upon rational intuitionism and Humean sentimentalism in our understanding of the practical powers of reason because it captures its internal relation to rational agency. This approach to interpreting Kant's novelty and continuing his legacy serves the purpose of reconceptualizing some crucial contemporary issues. Kant's critical rationalism is the preferable alternative to unsatisfactory options such as dogmatism and skepticism toward practical reason, empiricism and rationalism with respect to the source of the requirements of practical reasoning, as well as realism and antirealism about the primary function of ethical concepts.[14] Whether and to what extent this promise is fulfilled depends heavily on how the construction of reason is understood to function.

In Kant's view, practical reason is the capacity through which rational agents conceive of action and act on reasons: it denotes rational willing. While humans are capable of being willing rationally, unlike ideal rational beings, they do not have direct insight into practical truths. They determine what they ought to do through practical reasoning. In the process of reasoning about the right course of action, they start with what they know about themselves and with the general representations of the conditions of their rational agency. They then ask whether the proposals for action that come to mind pass the test of universality.

How exactly to apply such a test and whether it delivers what it promises remain hotly contested issues (Wood 2017). However, failures to deliver a system of duties do not necessarily mean that the CI lacks practical significance (Timmons 2015). Its main significance lies in the fact that practical reasoning is effective and transformative because and insofar as it is the correct form of self-government (Bagnoli 2021). Agents determine themselves as such via reasoning; in other words, self-representation as a rational agent has an impact on deliberation, which produces the moral incentive. Kant holds that respect (or reverence for the lawmaking capacity, in which the value of humanity consists) constitutes the only moral incentive (Kant C2 Ak 5.78, 76; see also MM Ak 6.399–402); this claim is at the core of an argument centered on moral experience.

1.2.4 The Appeal to Moral Experience

The efficacy of reason may be understood to be a *metaphysical* question insofar as it requires a demonstration of transcendental freedom. Kant holds that such a demonstration cannot be offered, since it would require us to step outside the bounds of reason, which we cannot transcend. Instead of undertaking this

---

[14] See also Korsgaard 2008, pp. 30–31, 55–57, 234, 310.

impossible task, he offers an argument for the efficacy of reason. In fact, a primary goal of the critique of practical reason is to show that the notion of the reason is objective insofar as it is effectively applicable to humans (C2 Ak 5: 156).

The method by which Kant proposes to defend the objectivity of practical reason is *critical* rather than dogmatic. The object of the rational critique is the empirical reason, which is prone to various distortions: it is often misled by natural desires and inclinations in the formation of the ends of action, and it may rely uncritically on belief. It therefore needs to be disciplined. The method of this discipline is reflexive: reason is deployed to criticize itself (C2 Ak 5.62 ff.). Arguably, the notion of construction helps dispel the "paradox of the method" by illustrating how the activity of reason unfolds. However, it remains unclear how to prove that human agents are indeed capable of making and being guided by rational constructions.

In the *Critique of Practical Reason*, Kant provides an obscure answer to the question of the efficacy of the moral law: it is a "fact of reason" that cannot be proven (C2 Ak 5.46–48). The term "fact" may be misleading, since it invites association with the epistemological model of moral perception which seems to commit to realism (Ameriks 2003). To avoid this misconception, many constructivists have discounted the role of the fact of reason in the general plan of the foundation of moral obligation (e.g., O'Neill 1989). Conversely, Rawls adopts this argument to show that ordinary moral experience coheres with the deliverances of the CI and concludes that Kant has developed "not only a constructivist understanding of practical reason but also a coherentist conception of its justification" (Rawls 1999, p. 524). Congruence with ordinary moral experience is an argument in favor of ethical objectivity; it proposes that pure practical reason manifests itself in human agency and that the moral law is effective as a form of authority, at least an implicit one, in ordinary human reasoning (Rawls 2000, p. 291).

There is, however, a plausible interpretation of the subjective aspect of the fact of reason that extends beyond this coherentist argument. Instead of an empirical fact, the fact of reason is a kind of self-awareness that arises under the guise of a moral feeling. Ordinary agents are aware of the authority of moral obligations in the form of a complex feeling of respect toward the capacity for self-legislation. This moral feeling explains how moral obligations are felt as first-personally binding. The feeling of reverence is not grounded in sensibility; instead, it is a priori in that it originates from the mere contemplation of the moral law. This explanation, therefore, does not subtract from the idea that the authority of moral obligations is categorical; in fact, the former reinforces the latter. In the account of the moral experience, the moral law is not presupposed by the same mechanisms as are the categories in the perceptual experience of an object in space. The moral law is a regulative ideal of rational agency. While failures to attain the moral law reveal that this is the *normative* ideal for humans, they do not prove that universality is not the norm constitutive of rationality. The experience that follows any such failure or violation demonstrates the extent to which such an ideal is ingrained in the human character.

Correspondingly, the fact of reason does not have the same epistemic *status* as a theoretical proposition, despite imposing itself with a force and an immediacy akin to those of a priori propositions. It is a "phenomenological" claim regarding the subjective feeling attending the performance of duty or its violation. While this argument is limited to the subjective authority of moral obligations, it plays a crucial role in the general case for the objectivity of moral obligation by showing that the ideal of rational and moral agency exerts categorical authority.

This argument exploits moral experience as exhibiting the *subjective authority* of moral obligation, and such experience constitutes the "subjective side" of the fact of reason. To this extent, it reveals a crucial aspect of the general plan – that moral categories do indeed apply to humans and rational requirements do guide them in action. Humans are sensitive to moral and natural incentives, despite repeatedly failing to properly attend to the moral law. Awareness of the authority of the moral law, nonetheless, is manifested in the moral feeling of respect. It is precisely this subjective awareness that guides action.

In this perspective, the argument regarding the fact of reason crucially integrates the account of the normative authority of practical reason with an explication of its subjective authority. Furthermore, it clarifies the sense in which a specific ideal of moral and rational agency may furnish "the basis" of the construction in the Kantian account of practical reasoning. The CI is a constitutive norm of reasoning that expresses a mode of self-reflection and self-representation.[15]

To say that the moral law is an idea of reason entails two other claims, namely that it is experienced *as a constraint* and that it is cannot be fully realized. In spite of these severe limitations, the argument from moral experience establishes that the moral law is nonetheless effective and can be approximated through practical reasoning.[16] Reasoning guided by the CI brings the moral law closer to common moral cognitions, and on this basis, it must then seek

---

[15] An alternative reading is that the core of the fact of reason consists in pure practical reason's consciousness of its own internal principles. For the view that practical reason provides the foundation for morality in a more robust sense than this, in line with "capacity first" methodology, see Schafer 2018, 2019a.

[16] This argument stands in stark contrast to sentimentalism, which grounds moral distinctions in sentiments and emotions. While some emotions concur with moral duty and sustain moral action, they are "merely analogous to moral feelings" and do not account for the efficacy of

confirmation in our ordinary moral experience. It is because we humans are endowed with a sensibility that we are susceptible to the moral incentive. If humans lacked moral sensitivity, they would be "morally dead" (MM Ak 6: 245). In particular, references to respect as the "only moral incentive" in ordinary moral thinking suffice to prove that moral categories are at work in human rational agents, albeit in a flawed manner.

Thus, the constructivist account of practical reason supports morality as a rational practice – not only of self-legislation and self-representation but also (and more importantly) of reorientation toward others, which commits us to think and act based on the guidance of universal reasons. Moral obligations are categorical, that is, they provide supremely authoritative reasons for acting independently of the actual desires and interests of an agent. There is a form of moral sensibility that is distinctive to the stance of rational agency; it is marked by respect for the moral law and, under this description, for the dignity of each individual. To this extent, the stance of rational and moral agency is also that of mutual accountability (cf. Darwall 2006). This interpretation vindicates the thesis that self-legislation is also a kind of sustained co-legislation with others represented as members of the kingdom of ends, and it substantiates the Kantian view of moral obligations as categorical imperatives.[17]

1.2.5 The Sovereignty of Practical Reason

These considerations may help situate Kantian constructivism in the contemporary debate about realism. Many interpret the argument regarding the fact of reason as an explicit commitment to moral realism insofar as it establishes that the moral law is imposed upon us prior to and independently of reasoning.[18] The main source of doubt toward the constructivist interpretation is that it does not support the objectivist ambitions of Kant's theory. The constructivist argument from the fact of reason is undermined by the lack of any evidence of an objective side (*ratio essendi*) underpinning the subjective side (*ratio cognoscendi*).

One option for resolving this controversy is to reconsider the *scope* of construction. In one interpretation, the construction concerns the very objects of rational choice, that is, the rational ends of action. In the other interpretation, it is limited to their authority. In the former case, rational agents identify the correct ends of action via reasoning and are thereby bound by

---

moral reasons (C2 Ak 5: 152). In fact, emotional motives detract from the moral value of actions conforming to moral duty.

[17] On the social dimension of the CI, see Reath 2006, pp. 173–95; Bagnoli 2017, 2021.

[18] Ameriks 2003; cf. Kleingeld 2010, pp. 55–72.

this construction; in the latter, the ends of action are correct irrespective of how rational agents may justify them, even though they become authoritative through reasoning. The former is more radical in that it allows practical reason to build the objects of will – that is, the rational ends of action – without relying on any prior ranking of values. It is doubtful that the latter, more modest interpretation can be compatible with the *autonomy of reason* (Engstrom 2009, p. 127). It gains plausibility only because the former and more radical understanding of construction is understood to be subjectivist. Neither Kant nor contemporary Kantian constructivists are subjectivists. The challenge, therefore, is to explain the role of subjective authority within the general objectivist plan.

The radical constructivist model takes Kant's humility regarding the bounds of reason at face value: a straightforwardly foundationalist argument based on the *ratio essendi* of the moral law seems utterly incompatible with Kant's assessment of such bounds. Nonetheless, this is not an admission that Kant has failed on his own grounds. Rather, the claim regarding the bounds of reason is best understood against the backdrop of Kant's assertion of the sovereignty of practical reason. The metaphor of construction is meant to capture the sovereignty of practical reason by illustrating the generative nature of reason and its capacity to produce its own objects. Owing to its reliance on moral psychology and anthropology, the constructivist account differs from a coherentist account of practical reason by entailing a full-fledged account of the moral powers at work in the activity of empirical practical reason. Constructivism embraces the view that without the support of moral psychology, ethical theory loses its practical relevance for humans, since it fails to justify its objectivist claims as applicable to beings such as ourselves.

Finally, with the proviso that realism and antirealism are terms of art, ineffectual in fully capturing the complexity of Kant's position, the constructivist characterization is more promising than others. If the moral law is an a priori principle of pure practical reason that neither implies nor acknowledges any other prerequisites, it is unclear how the claim commits to either realism or antirealism. The purported advantage of constructivism in capturing the Kantian claim lies in its account of the autonomy and self-certification of reason (O'Neill 2015, pp. 13–38). Kant's conception of practical reason is unique in that its critique operates according to standards internal to itself, that is, the constitutive standards of reason. The authority of reason is established through a legitimacy test rather than by appealing to external foundations. These claims are strictly related and account for the sovereignty of the practical function of reason.

1.3 Conclusion

In this section, we considered the promise and prospects of Kantian construct-ivism as an attempt to defend ethical objectivity. This form of constructivism appeals to Kant's distinctive account of reason as practical and authoritative. Like moral realism, Kantian constructivism is an objectivist approach to ethics; however, it differs from the former in that it views the objects of practical reason as neither prior to nor independent of itself; they are its tasks, determined through correct practical reasoning.

Furthermore, the theory is compatible with a reasonable pluralism of values, which means that there may be plural conceptions of the good life within the constraints of reason. Kantian constructivism need not deny that morality acknowledges a wide variety of specific practical reasons for action. There is an intrinsic relation between the profile of moral agents and the formal norms constitutive of practical reasoning. But this is not a relation of fit, and it does not curtail the richness of moral life or the diversity of moral reasons, nor does it prevent moral change and progress.[19] On the one hand, Kantian constructivism supports the view that, under further critical scrutiny, individuals are able and entitled to change their minds about what matters to them. On the other hand, the claim that rationality exhibits a formal structure appears to overlook the various contingencies that affect human life. Hence, we shall address this issue in the following section.

2 The Inescapability of Moral Reasons

While Kant's moral philosophy has strongly influenced the development of normative ethics, its entry into metaethical debates has been more uncertain and contested.[20] Many scholars recognize that Kant's methodological approach captures some features of ordinary moral discourse, namely the aspirations of moral judgments to objective and unconditional authority; nonetheless, there are persistent disagreements as to whether such features are indeed peculiar and distinctive of moral language (Foot 1972) and how they should be explained (Mackie 1977, pp. 24, 29). Furthermore, there is a large consensus that Kant's account is untenable insofar as it presupposes transcendental idealism, as well as an animated debate about whether and how a Kantian account can be substantiated without such presuppositions (Allison 2006; O'Shea 2006; Baiasu 2016; Schafer 2019a; Tenenbaum 2019).

---

[19] For a positive assessment of Kant's philosophy of history, its role in critical thought, and its capacity to vindicate moral progress, see Kleingeld 1995. These themes will be explored in Section 4.

[20] See Hill 1989, 2001, 2008; and Scanlon 1998.

There are three main reasons to dismiss a metaethics inspired by Kant. First, the Kantian conception of moral obligation purports to be a kind of "practical necessity" unlike causal or logical necessity, and it seems to commit us to an antinaturalist metaphysics (Mackie 1977). Second, the appeal to abstract universal principles of reason seems to lead to a formalistic ethics, which fails to guide ordinary agents in practice or otherwise lacks rigor in application. The constructivist interpretation has significantly diminished the force of these objections, although the norms of structural (i.e., internal and constitutive of) rationality remain the focus of a lively debate.

Finally, the twentieth-century debate about metaethics has remained largely hostile to theories of practical reason due to the difficulty in explaining how they constitute genuine theoretical alternatives to extant forms of realism and antirealism. Their novelties seem to depend on their distinctive moral psychology and the noninstrumentalist account of practical reasoning. This difficulty has been reinforced by a rigid, persistent view of the divide between the metaethical and normative levels of ethical theory despite Rawls' recommendations to the contrary, which were reviewed in Section 1.1.

Christine M. Korsgaard's seminal work, *The Sources of Normativity* (1996a), marks a turning point in this scenario. Its aim is to offer a general view of normativity that places the Kantian account of practical reason right at the center of the metaethical disputes. The question of normativity arises because human agents are self-reflective and require reasons to act. Reliance on reasons is a matter of necessity to these agents, but this is a mundane kind of necessity that arises from a natural feature of the mind. Correspondingly, the alleged objectivity and unconditional authority of ethical judgments are affirmed by exploiting the features of human rationality. Korsgaard defends a transcendental argument in support of the view that moral obligations are a matter of practical necessity in the mundane sense that they are *inescapable and mark the bounds of human identity.*

This is undoubtedly a drastic departure from Kant's own account of practical reason and practical necessity; nonetheless, Korsgaard further elaborates on the appeal to formal principles of rationality and sparks new debates on the constitution of rational agency.

2.1 The Criteria of the Inquiry

Korsgaard's goal is to vindicate the objectivity and normative authority of practical reasons. The first step in her inquiry into the nature of normativity is the characterization of moral concepts as tools "to talk about matters which for us are important in very deep, strong, and profound practical ways" (Korsgaard 1996a, p. 12). These facts about the psychological and practical effects of moral discourse determine the criteria of adequacy for any account of normativity, in the sense that any ethical theory must be answerable to them. First, they establish a criterion of *explanatory adequacy* for a theory of moral concepts. Second, they inquire whether the theory provides a plausible justification of the psychological and practical effects of moral practices and discourse: the criterion of *normative adequacy*. Explaining and justifying are two different tasks (Korsgaard 1996a, p. 16). The explanatory question concerns itself with how to account for the thought and conduct of intelligent animals, and it is addressed from the third-person standpoint of a spectator. By contrast, justification for the thoughts and actions of intelligent animals is a normative question addressed from the first-person standpoint, that is, the practical standpoint of an agent deliberating on how to act.

A successful theory of normativity has to fulfill three conditions. First, it must explain the phenomenon of radical disagreement over moral reasons; offer a normative justification from the agentive, first-person perspective; and provide reasons to skeptical, morally indifferent, or perplexed agents. Second, the explanation and justification of moral phenomena must be transparent and "[allow] us to act in the full light of knowledge of what morality is and why we are susceptible to its influences, and at the same time to believe that our actions are justified and make sense" (Korsgaard 1996a, p. 17). Finally, the answers to these questions must appeal to a sense of integrity and identity, effectively demonstrating that moral claims "issue in a deep way from our sense of who we are" (Korsgaard 1996a, p. 18).

While there may appear to be different kinds of normativity, Korsgaard believes that a unified account is possible (1996a, p. 21); she does not directly argue for this conclusion, but such an account emerges from her view of rational agency. Questions about the normativity of reasons arise in the case of autonomous agents, that is, those endowed with reflective capacities: "reflection reveals to us that the normativity of our values derives from the fact that we are animals of a certain type, moral and autonomous animals" (Korsgaard 1996a, p. 165).

Human agents represent themselves and others as self-reflective. This awareness is not a theoretical cognition (Korsgaard 1996a, p. 14); but a practical cognition at play in the act of practical judgment. As such, it does not necessitate any special metaphysical grounding, although it does require an explanation. The explanation is functional: this self-conception is the key to explaining not only the general phenomenon of normative authority but also the specific actions of individual agents based on reasons. Principles of reason can determine how individuals act because and insofar as these principles *express* the basic self-conceptions of the agents who respect them.[21]

2.2 Constructivism as Procedural Realism

Self-reflective agents seek reasons to act; such is the peculiar sense in which objectivity becomes a practical task for them. Korsgaard believes that this claim cannot be vindicated by engaging in metaethical debates about moral reality. Building upon Rawls's account, she provides a preliminary definition of constructivism in proceduralist terms, that is, the view that "there are answers to moral questions *because* there are correct procedures to get there" (1996a, p. 38). Unlike Rawls, however, she represents constructivism as a type of "procedural realism" according to which "there are correct procedures for answering moral questions *because* there are moral truths or facts that exist independently of such procedures and that such procedures track" (1996a, pp. 36–37). This is in contrast to "substantive realism," which holds that the criteria of objectivity for moral judgments are guaranteed by an external reality – by the facts of the world as it is – independently of the profile of rational agents. According to procedural realism, on the other hand, the criteria of objectivity are internal and dependent on the norms of rational agency and thus fully explicable against the background of the moral psychology of the relevant moral agents. The definition of metaethical constructivism in proceduralist terms captures an important axis of the debate (cf. Copp 2013, pp. 114, 117–18).

This mode of presenting the credentials of constructivism clarifies that substantive realism and constructivism share a view of moral obligations as objective, but they differ regarding the way in which objectivity is established as well as the role played by reasoning and, more broadly, by the ideals of practical rationality in their justification. This presentation highlights the comparative advantages of constructivism in terms of the criteria presented at the outset: constructivism exhibits marked explanatory advantages over its competitors. First, constructivism offers a straightforward argument in support of the intrinsic normativity of moral judgments that also serves as "a potentially devastating argument" against moral realism (Shafer-Landau 2003, p. 49). Second, it avoids any special ontology, and it is compatible with non-reductive naturalism (Enoch 2011, p. 324). Third, it provides an explanation for why something is deemed to be correct – showing an explanatory capacity which realism lacks (Shafer-Landau 2003, pp. 46, 51); hence, the realist proposal may sound like a mere "expression of confidence" (Korsgaard 1996a,

---

[21] "The principle or law by which you determine your actions is one that you regard as being expressive of *yourself*" (Korsgaard 1996a, p. 100).

p. 41) that marks a decisive inclination toward dogmatism. Finally, Kantian constructivism establishes a strong relation between rationality and morality, although there are persistent disagreements over the nature of such a connection (Brink 1992; Copp 2005; Smith 2015).

2.3 The Normative Question

By focusing on the normative question, Korsgaard takes over an argument originally formulated in support of moral realism, namely, G. E. Moore's *open question argument* (1996a, pp. 43, 124, 215, 218). Moore's argument is designed to eliminate all the theories that reduce moral judgments to judgments about natural or metaphysical properties (Moore 1903, p. x). Any such reduction is open to rational assessment and reasoned argument. According to Moore, this is because the moral domain consists of intrinsically normative entities that are irreducible to their natural and metaphysical properties.

While there are disagreements over the results of Moore's argument, its fortune in twentieth-century metaethics largely depends on its emotivist interpretation, which insists on the "magnetism" of ethical judgments. For noncognitivists, the naturalistic reduction fails because ethical judgments express conative and normative states instead of describing properties, and they thus require a nonrepresentational treatment (Stevenson 1937). In a similar vein, Korsgaard extends Moore's objection to all forms of moral realism, both naturalist and antinaturalist: "The move of the realist is to put an end to the regression by simply deciding it (by fiat): declaring that some things are intrinsically normative" (1996a, p. 33). Korsgaard agrees with antirealists that the postulation of unanalyzable and "brutely normative" properties is ontologically queer, fails to explain how inferential relations unfold, and leaves the normativity of basic ethical properties shrouded in mystery (Mackie 1977, pp. 38 ff.; Blackburn 1988; cf. Rosati 2016, pp. 209–10).

However, Korsgaard does not defend an expressivist semantics (2003, p. 122 n. 49). Her more radical plan is to "break with the platitudes of XX century metaethics," and thus, to distance herself from the disputes centered on the claim that the contents of ethical judgments are descriptive or otherwise "emotional expletives" (Korsgaard 2003, p. 105).[22] She maintains that

---

[22] Hussain and Shah hold that Korsgaard misunderstands metaethics, and that her views on normativity or first-personal authority can be argued from a noncognitivist view (Hussain and Shah 2006, pp. 93, 100; cf. Lenman 2012). Contrary to the latter remark, Korsgaard states that nothing can be gained by adopting an expressivist account of normativity (Korsgaard 2003, pp. 8–9). The argument in support of this choice is that noncognitivism represents normativity from a vantage point external to the practice. In general, this dismissal uncharitably equates expressivism with the view that ethical judgments are "emotional expletives." This line of

a philosophical theory of normativity cannot be pursued solely by reflecting on the nature of concepts and moral language but should rest on account of the workings of practical reason. Korsgaard argues that normative authority is the philosophical problem and that it should be addressed *in the first-person perspective* rather than with a special moral ontology. Both realism and expressivism are said to fall short of this criterion (Korsgaard, 1996a, 2008, pp. 30–31, 55–57, 67–68, 234).

Many scholars have noted that Korsgaard's argument fails to fully characterize constructivism in contrast to non-reductivist varieties of realism.[23] Some have also argued that Korsgaard's argument does nothing to advance the debate over the queerness of objectivist ethics insofar as the construction involves "acts of ex-nihilo creation" (Hussain and Shah 2006, pp. 290–92). These criticisms reiterate that Korsgaard fails to distinguish the questions on practical reason from the metaethical ones, but this point is not theoretically innocent since constructivism programmatically casts doubt on the very distinction between the metaethical and normative levels of ethical theory.

In general, this line of criticism underestimates the effects of the practical turn in the debate about objectivity. Shifting the question of ethical objectivity from the ontological to the practical dimension amounts to pressing the case that ontology is not the topic of interest here, and thus the viability of moral realism is not all that matters (cf. Copp 2013). Critics are correct in acknowledging the difficulty of identifying the distinctive features of Korsgaard's constructivism, but this is caused by two extraneous factors that do not undermine constructivism as such. First, Korsgaard's negative argument in support of constructivism largely coincides with a noncognitivist appraisal of the primary function of ethical concepts and judgments, which is said to be neither representational nor descriptive (2008, pp. 302 ff.); however, this is only part of the constructivist story. Second, the practical–theoretical distinction can be formulated such that it clarifies practical knowledge as a variety of self-knowledge instead of denying the cognitive function of practical reason (Bagnoli 2013; Engstrom 2013, p.139). By extension, some constructivists have defended constructivism as

---

argument underestimates the theoretical powers of expressivism as defended e.g., by Allan Gibbard.

[23] According to Hussain and Shah, Korsgaard does not differentiate between constructivism and anti-reductivist realism, because she overlooks the distinction between metaethics and normative ethics (2006, p. 265) and misunderstands metaethical tasks (2006, p. 293). Indeed, Korsgaard's argument has a more limited target than she intends, since her strain of constructivism is compatible with anti-reductivist realism (2006, pp. 272, 275 n. 14, 278). However, it is debatable whether her theory provides nothing distinctive or bases itself on a mere misunderstanding of the divide between metaethical and normative claims (2006, p. 286). Pushing this line of thought appears to be begging the question, since the aim of constructivism itself is to overcome the divide between metaethics and normative ethics.

a species of practical cognitivism that remains non-descriptivist and anti-representationalist but nonetheless commits itself to a full-fledged account of the powers of reason (Bagnoli 2013; Engstrom 2013; Schafer 2015a, 2015b).

Furthermore, Korsgaard produces no argument analogous to Kant's objection of heteronomy against neo-Humean theories. Korsgaard herself interprets Hume as deploying a constructivist method (Korsgaard 2008, pp. 263–301, 1996a, chapter 2), and her defense of agential autonomy in terms of the natural capacity of self-reflexivity attempts to improve upon Humean theories that explain away objectivity and normativity as phenomena that are all too human (O'Neill 1996, p. xii). Her improvement consists in vindicating the objectivity of normative claims by uncovering the way in which they are constructed. This constructivist account envisions moral reasons as practical ones whose force depends on features of human psychology.[24]

To wit, the formula for procedural realism establishes that moral truths are the results rather than the starting points of practical reasoning, but it cannot fully account for the constructive or generative function of reason. While the procedural formula of constructivism frames the question of ethical objectivity away from robust ontological assumptions about the moral domain, this is merely the beginning of a larger philosophical project.

2.4 The Argument from Practical Identity

The Kantian claim that practical judgments can be successfully grounded in practical reason has been met with disbelief in contemporary metaethics. Two major obstacles account for this hostility: the metaphysics entailed by this claim and its abstractness. Korsgaard's constructivism seems to sidestep the former since her view of practical reason is grounded in human nature.[25] The latter concern, however, is most formidable and raised with insistence.

Many scholars object that the capacity for reason is too abstract to provide substantive normative reasons; it seems more plausible to explicate the force and diversity of moral reasons in terms of cultural traditions and social practices. Finally, treating moral obligations as rational requirements does not put an end to the question about their normative authority (Broome 2005) unless rational requirements are either intrinsically normative in themselves or

---

[24] This definition concurs with the Humean account of practical reasons (Schroeder 2007, p. 1), despite potential further disagreement over the relevant psychological features (capacities, desires, wants, likes, and cares).

[25] On the other hand, this metaphysical abstinence may also be regarded as a cost, especially with respect to transcendental arguments, insofar as they are taken to commit to transcendental idealism, see Stern 2011; Baiasu 2016.

valuable independent of their contingent benefits. These charges can be met
only by vindicating the intrinsically normative nature of rationality.

These issues about the Kantian project are brought back to life by Bernard
Williams (1981, 1985), and they can be situated more broadly in the critique of
the Enlightenment tradition.[26] Moral authority seems to be a matter of special
relations and loyalties determined by a system of blame rather than by abstract
ideals of equal standing. By treating moral obligations as requirements of bare
reason, Kantians strip them of normative authority and motivational force
(Williams 1981, 1985, 1994). This is apparent in the case of conflicts between
the moral duty to respect humanity on the one hand and special bonds, affec-
tions, loyalties, projects, and ambitions on the other. Consider the dilemma
between saving your beloved spouse and a complete stranger when you are
forced to choose one of the two – does bare reason have enough authority to
provide a stance from which to assess this conflict? The answer depends heavily
on the conception of reason and of its scope.

Williams puts forth the case that the standpoint of bare reason is *emptied* of
content and thus lacks the driving force that characterizes particular normative
reasons for action. In his view, if the stance of rational agency is freestanding
and invulnerable to external authorities, it must also be insensitive to special
bonds and ties, but then the mechanism through which it can provide guidance
to agency becomes a mystery. Furthermore, the ideal of autonomy rests on the
presumption that the rational agent can choose the normative standards of action
all by himself, independently of any social practice or the tradition and culture
in which he belongs. This pretense is implausible because it requires freedom
from the constraining effects of the social environment that human agents do not
possess. It is also a misguided ideal of self-sufficiency and self-reliance that
proves to be self-defeating: by disconnecting the individual from his social and
cultural roots, it deprives ordinary agents of the knowledge of their places and
roles in the communities to which they belong. The phenomenon of "practical
necessity" – the volitional features that render some actions impossible without
that the identity of the person seriously alters – involves social embedding and
special loyalties (Williams 1993 p. 101).

With sociality in focus, other aspects of the normative nature of morality
begin to emerge. One is that morality exerts a *coercive function* by virtue of the
prescriptive aspects of moral judgment as well as the normative pull of social
emotions such as shame and blame (Gibbard 1990). The authority of morality

---

[26] This critique resonates with the communitarian critique of the ideal of autonomy, which is
regarded as individualistic and misguided in that it promotes self-sufficiency and severs the links
between the agent and the community to which she belongs. Related issues on the historical
formations of practical reason and identity will be addressed in Section 4.

pertains to social tools for enforcing compliance and uniformity instead of the rational exercise of self-governance. This is another sense in which self-governance is not only an issue in moral psychology but also a central topic in metaethics.

This debate reveals a deep tension within morality that appears to comprise a complex and layered cluster of phenomena. Understanding morality and its relation to other normative practices and concepts is a central metaethical task (Wood 1995, pp. 234, 249). Korsgaard's goal is to make decisive progress in this dispute by importing the notion of "practical identity," that is, "a description under which you value yourself, a description under which you find your life to be worth living and your actions to be worth undertaking" (1996a, p. 101, cf. 2009, p. 20). This concept then becomes the focus of the investigation of normativity: "Your reasons express your identity, your nature; your obligations spring from what your identity forbids" (Korsgaard 1996a, p. 101). The normativity of obligations and, more generally, of normative claims is rooted in one's nature and identity as an agent. More precisely, the normative force of these obligations and claims derives from volitional necessities, which demarcate the boundaries of one's identity as an agent: "Unless you are committed to some conception of your practical identity, you will lose your grip on yourself as having any reason to do one thing rather than another – and with it, your grip on yourself as having any reason to live and act at all" (Korsgaard 1996a, p. 120).

Korsgaard's response acknowledges an important point in Williams' approach to morality and identity – that human agents are *social*: "Human beings are social animals in a deep way. It is not just that we go in for friendship or prefer to live in swarms or packs. The space of linguistic consciousness – the space in which meanings and reasons exist – is a space that we occupy together" (1996a, p. 145, cf. 1996b, pp. 275–310, 188–223). While this may be a significant concession to the social critique of Kant's moral theory, it is not a complete surrender.[27] In fact, this move allows Korsgaard to prove the derivative normative force of cultural and social bonds:

> But this reason for conforming to your particular practical identities is not a reason that springs from one of those particular practical identities. It is a reason that springs from your humanity itself, from your identity simply as a human being, a reflective animal who needs reasons to act and to live. And so it is a reason you have only if you treat your humanity as a practical, normative, form of identity, that is, if you value yourself as a human being (1996a, p. 121).

---

[27] Here, again, we may register a point of departure from Kant, since there is a social dimension to Kant's ethics, though its resources are not fully exploited by all varieties of Kantian constructivists, cf. Bagnoli 2017.

The answer to the skeptical worry takes the form of a transcendental argument. A necessary condition for the possibility of action is an unconditional principle or value rooted in the human identity as such. In order to take any action at all, individuals must value their humanity:

> Rational action exists, so we know it is possible. How is it possible? And then by the course of reflections in which we have just engaged, I show you that rational action is possible if and only if human beings find their own humanity to be valuable. But rational action is possible, and we are the human beings in question. Therefore, we find ourselves to be valuable (Korsgaard 1996a, pp. 123–24).[28]

It is *not* contingent that an agent be governed by some conception of practical identity or by some project. Instead of directly providing substantive normative reasons, local and contingent identities do so only if and insofar as they are coherent with humanity (Korsgaard 1996a, p. 121). Human agents find themselves with various kinds of identities arising from their cultures, roles, and positions. Not all of them are valuable, and the determination of their respective value is a normative question arising in the first-person perspective, that is, in the agent's stance.

It is critical to note here that *the agent's stance is reflective* and does not coincide with whatever the agent happens to be or to will at any given moment. Rather, the stance of reflection is such that the agent critically reviews any state of mind and proposal of action. This reflective scrutiny allows for autonomy as self-governance. To explain how this ideal of autonomy operates for ordinary agents who enter into reflection with multiple social identities and practical concerns, Korsgaard introduces a concept alien to Kant's conceptual vocabulary – that of "endorsement."[29] Borrowed from Harry Frankfurt, this concept names the mechanism by which the particular identities *become* normative and authoritative for the agent. The mechanism is meant to explain how the agent's stance is formed insofar as it identifies what the agent finds important, cares for, and values.[30]

---

[28] Korsgaard's phrasing often switches from "human identity" to "rational identity" or "identity as a rational agent"; and it is sometimes ambiguous whether it is humanity that must be valued, or practical rationality, or agency as such.

[29] Korsgaard attributes the "reflective endorsement of our nature" to Shaftesbury and David Hume (1996a, chapter 2, cf. 2008, pp. 263–301).

[30] For Frankfurt, endorsement represents the way in which the will takes shape; but it is not necessarily deliberated or reasoned (2004, pp. 97, 126), nor is it in service of morality (2006). Thus, in its original deployment, the concept of endorsement is central to an account of autonomous agency that is not merely alien but also decisively hostile to Kantian theory, since it denies that (i) agential autonomy rests on the autonomy of reason: that (ii) the rational will is practical reason; and that (iii) self-governance takes the form of self-legislation and warrants

For Korsgaard, the mechanism of endorsement does its job only to the extent that it is reflective and guided by rational standards (1996a, pp. 102, 108–09). Instead of a generic reflexive psychological mechanism that characterizes minds capable of making themselves the object of avowals or disavowals, it names only the normative activity governed by rational standards. To reflectively endorse a social identity does not amount to embracing any such identity reflexively; rather, it means accepting it on principled reasons, that is, under the scrutiny of reason. Rational scrutiny dictates that the mechanism of endorsement functions not merely as a test of *internality* (i.e., screening what pertains to the will or falls outside its bounds) but also as a test of rational *legitimacy* (i.e., determining whether it can be justified on the basis of reasons that can be shared among all).[31] The resulting picture is that rational agents have gained concreteness, but their characters, social identities, personal histories, loyalties, projects, and relations provide them with normative reasons only to the extent that they are rationally justified. Reflection allows for self-governance because it bears a universalist structure, namely the CI. Correspondingly, the appropriate form of self-government is self-legislation (Korsgaard, 1996a, pp. 36, 91, 231–32, cf. 2008, p. 3), which commits to take others into account, since "only if the law ranges over every rational being ... [then] the resulting law will be the moral law" (Korsgaard 1996a, p. 99). Thus, the universal form of principles aims to establish not merely the internal individual consistency of individuals but also the coherence of an ideal community of rational agents having equal normative standing.

This is a controversial claim.[32] On the one hand, the appeal to the mere form of the law appears insufficient for grounding substantive moral reasons.[33] On the other hand, the requirement that reasons range over all rational beings seems too demanding for individual self-governance and unnecessarily restrictive as an explanation of the authority of nonmoral normative claims.

Moreover, there are reasons to doubt that the introduction of the device of reflective endorsement represents a decisive improvement on the traditional defense of the authority of morality. A related concern is that the imported

---

moral integrity. In short, endorsement is a generic device to settle the bounds of the will, and an agent may self-govern without possessing moral integrity.

[31] "To act on a reason is already, essentially, to act on a consideration whose normative force may be shared with others" (Korsgaard 1996a, p. 136).

[32] On Korsgaard's conception of self-legislation, see Cohen 1996, p. 170; Wood 1999, p. 156. For an alternative account of the complementarity of self-legislation and co-legislation, see Bagnoli 2017.

[33] For the critique that the logical norm of coherence cannot be the source of substantial reasons, see Williams 1996; Gibbard 1999; Smith 1999; Cholbi 1999. In some formulations, this critique underappreciates the distinction between the categorical imperative and a norm of logical consistency (cf. O'Neill 1975, 1989; Engstrom 2009; Bagnoli 2021).

notion of reflective endorsement may not be successfully integrated. It creates a tension that threatens to undermine the entire constructivist project. The work of reflective endorsement can be taken to be "constructive" in that it builds the contents of objective and authoritative reasons for action. However, it obscures the role and status of universality in accounting for the normative authority of reason. The transcendental argument directly addresses the general worry about how to ground substantial normative claims in abstract norms of rational agency, but it remains unclear what it means that its compellingness is demonstrated by the power of reflection if this equates to reflective endorsement.[34] Korsgaard purports to exploit a rather plain and modest conception of reflection to show how agents are bound by reasons and moral obligations, but the worry is that this is not sufficient to sustain her transcendental argument.[35]

2.5 The Reflective Stance and the Stance of Agency

By appropriating the notion of reflective endorsement, Korsgaard moves away from the problematic implications of Kant's account of the autonomy of reason. However, this move generates false expectations regarding the desired type of autonomy or self-government as well as the normative phenomena to be vindicated. The risk of confusion is particularly high, as Korsgaard's discussion of the normative question oscillates between the stance of *reflection* and that of deliberation. The former stance is one representative of the agent, and in a way, the possibility of the normative question pertains essentially to this stance. This means that normative questions about what there is reason to do arise for agents endowed with reflective minds, although such agents do not necessarily need reasons in order to act. If so, then the relation between reasons and agency is yet to be established.

In asserting that universality is the norm of reflection, Korsgaard rejects *subjectivist voluntarism*, that is, the view that normative authority depends on a subjective choice of the individual agent (1996a, pp. 21–27). By contrast, for Korsgaard, self-legislation does not entail that agents are bound by the law because or insofar as they produce it, nor does it entail that the moral law is authoritative only insofar as it is endorsed (1996a, pp. 234–35, cf. 2008,

---

[34] Schafer argues that the prospects of the Kantian constitutivist strategy rest on a more fundamental commitment to "capacities-first philosophy," that is, a method of philosophical inquiry which regards our basic, self-conscious rational capacities as fundamental (Schafer 2019a). For further considerations concerning the persuasiveness of the constitutivist strategy, see Tubert (2010) and Baiasu (2016). Tenenbaum (2019) argues that the constitutivist argument leaves open varieties of worries about alienation from constitutive norms, and defends a form of constitutivism that relies on more robust starting points than Korsgaard's.

[35] Some critics assume that the role of the value of humanity in such arguments seems to commit one to moral realism, see e.g., Stern 2011, 2013; Fitzpatrick 2013.

pp. 207–29). Korsgaard defends the CI as a constitutive norm of reasoning that applies to all rational beings rather than a singular decree of any particular agent (1996a, pp. 36, 234–36).

However, when discussing deliberation through the model of reflective endorsement, the emphasis shifts to individual choice and the source of normativity then appears to become the agent's concern with his own integrity and identity: "values are created by human beings" as "a matter of making laws" (1996a, p. 112).[36] The conclusion to the process of reflection grounds action in the "moral identity" under which the agent finds her life "to be worth living" and her actions "worth undertaking" (Korsgaard 1996a, p. 101). Self-legislation is the highest form of self-government and aims to foster moral integrity and practical identity.

The resulting view is that "An obligation always takes the form of a reaction against a threat of a loss of identity" (Korsgaard 1996a, p. 102). This focus on integrity in a project on the rational grounds of moral obligations has been widely criticized. Critics argue that some of the original insights provided by Kant's model are lost since rational agents seem to be oriented toward others out of concern for their own integrity, coherence, and identity instead of cognizance of others' claims or responsiveness to others' demands (Skorupski 1998; Bird-Pollan 2011, p. 377; cf. Korsgaard 2011). Korsgaard's belief that morality and agential integrity are tightly related seems to be misguided if moral obligations spring from the moral claims and demands of others (Cohen 1996; Williams 1996; Wallace 2019, p. 46).[37] These worries originate in a failure to appreciate that on the Kantian view, reasons are not private (cf. Korsgaard 1996a, p. 136, 1996b, p. 301), and "respect for others" is not specular but complementary to "respect for oneself": one cannot truly respect oneself unless one recognizes others as having equal standing (cf. Korsgaard 1996b, pp. 188–224). Once this claim is fully developed, the objections mentioned earlier are not fatal, but these resources are underplayed in Korsgaard (1996a).

Korsgaard also identifies reflective endorsement as the basic mechanism of rational agency. She says that "our capacity to turn our attention on to our own mental activities is also a capacity to distance ourselves from them, and to call them into question" (1996a, pp. 92–93). However, reflective distance does not explain action; the bridge from reflection to action is endorsement. If rational action is explained by endorsement, then authority is reduced to psychological

---

[36] While Korsgaard takes this view to coincide with Kant's (1996a, p. 236), the latter distinguishes between the legislator and the author of the law (see MM Ak 6: 227).

[37] A different but related worry is that modeling moral agency on personal integrity without reference to social practices is risky in that it carries a propensity toward self-indulgence and moral arrogance, see Williams 1993, p. 100.

pressure. Instead, if reflection assumes all the philosophical work of explaining rational action, then the metaphor of reflective distance is inadequate to capture rational agency (cf. Korsgaard 2008, §7.5.1). Reflection does more than merely achieve "reflective distance" (Korsgaard 1996a, pp. 129, 229–31); it also affords the principle constitutive of rational action.

The appeal to the CI as the constitutive norm of rationality and the model of endorsement are two different strategies for answering the question of normativity, and they stand for different conceptions of autonomous choice. They converge only on the assumption that reflection takes the form of universality. But the dual process of reflective distancing and endorsement does not commit to any form or structure of rational agency. In fact, this two-stage account becomes redundant once the constitutivist tenet is established. If the CI as the constitutive norm of reasoning is in place, it renders the appeal to reflective endorsement dispensable. The constitutivist argument, which appeals to the constitutive rational norms, is sufficient to ground the normativity of practical reasons.

2.6 The Constitutivist Strategy against Moral Skepticism

In Korsgaard's view, the principles of practical reason are constitutive of autonomous action in the sense that they are not external constraints or restrictions, but "*describe* the procedures involved in rational willing. But they also function as normative or guiding principles, because in following these procedures we are guiding ourselves" (2008, p. 31). Second, the constitutive norms of practical reason are also norms of self-constitution: "In order to be a person – that is, to have reasons – you must constitute yourself as a particular person, and [. . .] in order to do that, you must commit yourself to your value as a person-in-general, that is, as a rational agent" (Korsgaard 2009, p. 25).[38] Rational action is expressive of the identity of the agent *as a whole*, rather than at the service of particular preferences and desires seeking to be satisfied, and this is how the action becomes attributable and imputable to the agent (Korsgaard 2008, p. 101).

This means that the CI is constitutive of the stance of rational agency. The integrity necessary for the rational agent cannot be guaranteed except through abiding by the moral law (Korsgaard 2009, p. xii, chapter 3, 2019). The principle of instrumental reason is also a constitutive principle of agency, in the sense that it provides agents with a will (2008, p. 92), but its normative

---

[38] Korsgaard 2008, 2009, 2019. On some problematic aspects of the Kantian move from constructivism to self-constitution, and the attempt to derive the moral law, see Fitzpatrick 2013; Guyer 2013.

authority depends on the basic authority of the noninstrumental principle of rationality (2008, pp. 67–68).[39] This is because the CI by itself commits to its realization, and thus it includes prescriptions about the means to achieve the end. To this extent, the principle of instrumental reason is not separable from the CI, but it is best understood as an aspect of it, which warrants its efficacy. Thus, the proper conclusion of Korsgaard's argument is that there is only one principle of practical reason, and this is the CI.

This ambitious argument positions Kantian constructivism as a viable option within the debate about agential authority and self-governance, in dialogue with the philosophy of action, and hence beyond the theory of moral obligations. It aims to explain how practical reasons, in general, get a grip on agents. In short, Korsgaard's argument responds to moral skepticism as a form of skepticism about rational agency, and since agency is inescapable, moral skepticism therefore becomes irrational. Korsgaard's general claim is that "constitutive standards meet skeptical challenges to their authority with ease" (2009, p. 29, subsection 1.4.2). Furthermore, it establishes that "it is not imperfection that places us under rational norms, but freedom, which brings with it the needed possibility of resistance to, as well as compliance with, these norms" (Korsgaard 2008, p. 52 n. 39).

A general issue surrounding constitutivism is that, if there were norms constitutive of rationality, it would be impossible to violate them without losing the status of rationality. If this is the case, then such norms would be definitional rather than normative, and they would exclude the possibility of error (Lavin 2004; cf. Korsgaard 2008, p. 60).[40] Korsgaard's strategy to address this issue is to distinguish kinds of failures in conforming to the constitutive norms as defective approximations (2009, pp. 159–76, 45–49). The issue at stake, however, is whether such defective approximations count as transgressions of normative requirements *for* agents and not merely as defects of what is required *of* agents. This suggestion demands a more radical strategy, which explains how a constitutivist metaphysics of capacities explains why error counts as an imperfection of an action (Fix 2020) and maps varieties of modes of alienation from constitutive norms (Tenenbaum 2019).

The constitutivist strategy is invoked to address two levels of questions: that of general normativity and specific normativity of particular obligations. To a certain extent, the constitutivist strategy to explain the objectivity and authority of morality transforms the question "why be moral?" into "why be a rational

---

[39] For an earlier statement of this view, O'Neill 1989, pp. 73–74.

[40] Lavin's argument assumes that, since it is no accident that ideal agents uphold sound norms, it must have been impossible for them to violate such norms; but it is arguable that this assumption is false, cf. Cokelet 2008.

agent?." This strategy, however, assumes that being a rational agent is an inescapable commitment rooted in the human condition. Indeed, Korsgaard's argument starts with the presumption that agency is a necessary condition of humanity, or in a more existentialist formulation, "human beings are *condemned* to choice and action" (2009, p. 1).

David Enoch (2006) points to a missing step in the constitutivist argument: the constitutivist strategy cannot be convincing unless we have a prior reason to be agents. First, it has to be demonstrated that some aims, motives, or capacities constitute agency. Second, it must be established that agency is a game in which we all have a reason to participate (insofar as we are humans). However, this is "a paradigmatically normative judgement" (Enoch 2006, p. 186), and its centrality shows that constructivism does not provide a full picture of normativity: it ultimately succeeds by appealing to an unconstructed presumption about the inescapability of agency. The corollary is that the promise of the success of the constitutivist strategy depends on the plausibility of moral realism (Enoch 2006, pp. 187, 192). The conclusion of Korsgaard's argument can be questioned by the mere conceivability of an agent who is indifferent to self-constituting in action and would be happy to label himself as a "shmagent." Shmagents fail Korsgaard's criteria of agency, and they are not moved by the threat of disintegration.

The ensuing discussion clarifies some distinct senses in which agency can be considered inescapable, albeit in a more modest sense than Korsgaard assumes. Even if all the particular enterprises were suspended, as in the process of radical assessment, some basic form of agency remains arguably ongoing because the process of radical assessment itself counts as a form thereof (Ferrero 2008 pp. 308–09, 2019). These considerations offer multiple ways of thinking the inescapability of agency. In this light, radical skepticism about agency is a logical possibility, but agency is inevitable for beings with the cognitive and conceptual capacities typical of humans. Korsgaard's argument seems to suggest that what vindicates these capacities for autonomous agency is that we care about them (cf. Rosati 2003, p. 522). Being constitutive of agency renders the relevant motives and capacities non-arbitrary; it would be self-defeating to challenge the capacities and motives that constitute agency, giving them a self-vindicating status (Velleman 2004b, pp. 290–91).

2.7 Conclusion

Korsgaard relocates the relevant notion of practical necessity and agential autonomy within the bounds of human nature. In contrast to Kant's account of practical necessity, she recognizes a significant element of contingency in the construction of practical reasons:

> Kant urges us to take things to be important because they are important to us. And this means that we must do so in full acceptance of the fact that what specifically is important to us is at bottom contingent and conditional, determined by biological, psychological, and historical conditions that themselves are neither justified nor unjustified, but simply there (Korsgaard 1996a, p. 242).

The main worry is that by doing so, Korsgaard fails to provide the robust defense of objectivity and authority that she promises (Cohen 1996, p. 173; Nagel 1996, p. 204).

The appeal to the inescapability of agency is meant to preempt the objection moved by Enoch (2006, section 5, pp. 185–87). But the ambiguity of the notion of necessity invoked represents a weakness in Korsgaard's general argument (cf. Enoch 2006, p. 188). While Korsgaard affirms that action is necessary (1.1.1), albeit neither logically nor causally, at times, she seems to defend the *psychological inevitability* of action, cashed out in existentialist overtones: "The claim that reason seeks the unconditioned is not based on an analysis of the abstract concept of reason. It is more a claim about the plight of self-conscious beings who because we are self-conscious need reasons to believe and to act" (1998, p. 61; see §1.3.4). The weak notion of volitional necessity, which becomes inevitable if its alternative is unthinkable, pertains to the bounds of human psychology rather than the constitutive features of reason (Herman 2008, p. 173; Fitzpatrick 2013, p. 43).

Nonetheless, her theory brings into sharp relief the relation between moral obligations and practical reason as a core topic in metaethics by refurbishing transcendental arguments against skepticism. Her work urges metaethical inquiry to focus on unresolved and even largely unexplored questions about rational agency. Criticisms of her transcendental argument for the inescapability of moral reasons have major implications for the debate about metanormativity.

In the words of Enoch, "deliberative inescapability or (the unavoidability of deliberation) can help us show that the deliberative indispensability is in no way less respectable than explanatory indispensability, so that arguments from deliberative indispensability work if inferences to the best explanations do" (2006, p. 195). These considerations encourage us to turn toward constructivist theories of rational deliberation, which take the problem of contingency upfront.

3 The Contingency of Moral Agreement

Our lives as rational and moral agents are severely marked by circumstantial contingencies beyond our individual control. In Kantian theories such as

Korsgaard's, the contingency of our biological, psychological, and historical conditions does not determine us one way or another, and it should not be regarded as an external constraint on valuing or a source of value. Rather, it is itself the object of choice: "Contingency itself is something that may either be actively embraced or passively endured, and this makes all the difference: the mature attitude is the one that actively embraces it, not the one that passively endures it [. . .] Kantian agents transform contingent values into necessary ones by valuing the humanity that is their source" (Korsgaard 1996a, p. 242). The very activity of reason perpetuates such transformations, and it is thought to be conducive to integrity and moral cohesion, in stark contrast to a precarious *modus vivendi*.

But the method through which this conclusion is derived can be disputed with regard to the status of the norms of rationality. Are the constitutive norms of rationality invulnerable to contingency? Moreover, are they sufficiently robust to warrant universal agreement on a core set of substantive principles of morality? If not, can such agreement be stably warranted on the basis of other, more contingent factors?

This section devotes itself to explaining the novelty and promise of Humean constructivism in addressing the implications of contingency that have eluded Kantian theories. Supporters of this view draw on various aspects of David Hume's legacy, offering a rather variegated cluster of views. The unifying tenet across this cluster is the negative claim that Kantian constructivism under-appreciates the contingency of morals and rationality: "If Humean meta-ethical constructivism is correct, then morality does not follow from pure practical reason, understood as the standpoint of a valuer as such. Instead, we must conceive of our relationship with morality as more contingent than that" (Street 2012, p. 55). Humeans abandon transcendental arguments and press for an alternative definition of the practical stance as the standpoint of contingency-ridden agents. Acknowledging the importance of contingency to our life leads us to forgo the Kantian aspirations to practical necessity and objectivity under the pressure of debunking arguments, some of which appeal to evolutionary explanations of ethics. In some of its varieties, the loss in objectivity is not an unbearable cost. Other varieties of Humean constructivism attempt, instead, to vindicate a broad conception of ethical objectivity by appealing to a general core of moral principles grounded in human nature.[41]

3.1 The Evaluative Standpoint

Sharon Street offers the most thorough defense of Humean constructivism (2006, 2008a, 2010), which decisively qualifies as antirealist and

---

[41] For an earlier formulation of Humean constructivism, see Bagnoli 2002, p. 121.

anticognitivist, although what makes it distinctive is less clear. Her negative argument for Humean constructivism targets both moral realism, insofar as it assumes a fixed and absolute moral ontology, and Kantian constructivism, to the extent that it relies on transcendental strategies. Both these theories underestimate the key role of contingency in the evaluative activities of human agents. Street reformulates the problem that constructivism is designed to answer into the following target question: how do truths about value enter into the world? She argues that the origin and nature of value should be explained in terms of the basic attitudes of living beings, which are radically contingent: "Causal forces, evolutionary and otherwise, gave rise to conscious living things capable of valuing things – whether it be food or their bodily integrity or each other – and with this state of mind of 'valuing' came truths about what is valuable – truths which hold from within the point of view of creatures who are already in that state" (Street 2012, p. 40). According to Street (2008b), evolutionary accounts of ethics have debunking effects, which undermine the plausibility of realism and threaten Kantian constructivism insofar as it relies on the absoluteness of the value of humanity.[42]

Distance from Kantian constructivism can be measured with respect to three foci of disagreement: (a) the powers of practical reason; (b) the place of morality in our lives; and (c) the methods of philosophical argumentation. While the main focus of the debate is the second of these (Street 2012, p. 41), the real disagreement concerns the underlying idea of reasoning as a "practical" pursuit.

On the surface, Street agrees with the Kantian claim that it is sufficient to offer a formal characterization of the practical standpoint, but this is defined as the perspective taken by any creature capable of the "valuing" state of mind. While Kantians render the formal characterization in terms of the structural norms of rationality, Street aims to provide a metaethical account of "valuing as such," that is, an explication of the attitude of valuing which does not itself presuppose any substantive values (2012, p. 40). First, the norms constitutive of valuing are logical consistency and means-ends coherence. Violating these requirements is not equivalent to committing any normative mistake; it amounts to merely failing to value (Street 2012). Second, the role of constitutive norms is explicative of the very activity of valuing rather than normative. Third, while these norms explicate what counts as valuing, they do not filter the contents of judgments about what is valuable; almost anything can be included in the practical standpoint.

---

[42] For a review of debunking arguments, see Vavova (2014). For a reply on behalf of realism, see Copp (2008); cf. Street (2008b). Tropman (2014) holds that constructivism shows no comparative advantages over moral realism in response to debunking arguments; for the contrary view that constructivism wields decisive resources to eschew debunking arguments by conceiving of objectivity as "a test of time," see Bagnoli 2019.

Street maintains that the CI is too rich to qualify as the governing principle of a formal construction because and insofar as it operates on the assumption that humanity has absolute value and makes morality necessary or inescapable. Thus, Kantian constructivists such as Korsgaard do not "ultimately remain true enough to the central constructivist point that there are no facts about normative reasons apart from the standpoint of an agent who is already taking things to be reasons" (Street 2012, p. 48).

The disagreement over the norms or requirements constitutive of the practical standpoint stems from a deeper debate regarding the power of transcendental arguments in general, particularly the ones appealing to the value of humanity. This controversy concerns the methods of philosophical argumentation that are apt to demonstrate the objectivity and necessity of moral truths, in contrast to contingent individual attitudes and biases. Street's argument questions the validity of the transcendental arguments and their place in a constructivist metaethics.[43]

Street attacks Korsgaard's view that our identity as human beings is more fundamental than other identities.[44] Recall that humanity in Kantian jargon is not a biological category but a practical one, which refers to embodied agents endowed with rationality (Kant MM 6:435; cf. Korsgaard 1996a, p. 123). Street challenges the relevance and adequacy of this category as marked by the feature of reflexivity (2012, p. 47). She objects that, by insisting on the allowance of a critical distance that is tantamount to the capacity for rational criticism, one is abandoning the practical standpoint and looking upon it as if from the outside, "thereby robbing the question of the standards that could make the question make sense" (2012, p. 49).

This objection echoes the critical points about the stance of agency raised in Section 2. However, it is questionable whether Street's characterization of the practical standpoint suffices for a radical alternative to Korsgaard regarding the conditions required to stop the regress in the demand for rational justification:

> On the Humean constructivist view I am proposing, then, the regress of normative questions comes to an end not with any substantive value, but with an understanding of the exact moment at which normative questions cease to make sense – namely, the moment one divorces oneself from the practical point of view altogether, refusing, for that moment, to take any value for granted (2012, p. 52).

Ultimately, the matter of contention concerns the character of the norms of structural rationality. By claiming that such norms are not merely instrumental,

---

[43] Street 2012, p. 55. A contested issue is the extent to which constructivists can avail themselves of transcendental arguments without a robust metaphysics, see Baiasu 2016, 2020; Schafer 2019a.

[44] Street 2012, pp. 45, 48.

Korsgaard concludes that the condition of the possibility of valuing is that persons themselves are of value.[45] As a counterexample, Street offers the hypothetical case of social animals that can categorically attribute value to something and engage in cooperative interactions for the sake of intrinsic values without valuing themselves. The conclusion of the thought experiment is a straightforward denial of Korsgaard's claim that valuing something commits one to value oneself (and others) on pain of incoherence. As a matter of coherence, one could value something without valuing oneself as its source (Street 2012, pp. 53, 55). It follows that the value of humanity cannot be taken to constitute the valuing attitude as such. Thus, the mistake is to assume that moral requirements must bind us independently of the evaluative standpoint itself (Street 2012, p. 56). Unlike the foundationalist view of rational justification, the constructivist view regards the regress stopper not as a substantive value but as a claim about structural rationality that must be value-neutral.

Kantian constructivists may reply that invoking the value of humanity as constitutive of the practical standpoint does not entail any values prior to or independent of undertaking such a standpoint: this dependence is conveyed by the metaphor of construction, which requires the method to be internal and constitutive of the exercise of reasoning. Understood as such a method, the CI serves as a constraint, and it excludes some contents as incompatible with a universal legislation; but this operation does not amount to *deriving* moral conclusions from descriptive premises. The role of the CI is not to select preconstituted options, as in other kinds of theories for which obligations are external constraints and restrictions. This is a genuine difference between constructivist and other accounts of the norms constitutive of reasoning.

This reply points to a question about what is distinctive to Street's antirealism and what the metaphor of construction achieves in her theory. First, construction appears to take on the work that Humean expressivists attribute to the projection of sentiments (Mackie 1977; Blackburn 1988). This is certainly a legitimate means of relying on Hume's legacy, but its similarity to Humean expressivism warrants closer scrutiny. We will come back to this question in Section 3.6.[46]

Second, Street's definition of metaethical constructivism assimilates the method of reflective equilibrium,[47] which justifies judgments of reasons holistically by considering all normative judgments, with the norms of consistency

---

[45] Street 2012, p. 53. For an analogous objection, see Lenman 1999, p. 167; Ridge 2012.

[46] Street insists on making a distinction between desiring and valuing in an attempt to differentiate her view from expressivism, but this strategy is insufficient to establish her point. For a critique of quasi-realism as an affirmation of mind dependency, see Street 2011.

[47] Cf. Rawls 1971; cf. O'Neill 2003; Scanlon 2002.

and coherence acting as constraints. Normative inquiry is akin to repairing Neurath's boat, one piece at the time. However, Street also claims that this account of normative inquiry is of "constitutive significance." James Lenman objects that constructivism is a method for figuring out substantive reasons, and thus it cannot simultaneously provide an analysis of what it means for something to be a reason; hence, it cannot play the role that Street claims.[48] This objection does not seem fatal to Street's position (see Southwood 2018, n. 5), but it certainly adds to a general concern over the coherence of a global metaethical constructivism regarding all practical reasons (Enoch 2009; Scanlon 2012).

A deeper worry arises about the normativity of the "formal" requirements that Street takes to be constitutive of valuing as such. As anticipated, Street narrows the domain of the constitutive norms of reasoning to those of logic. How do such requirements exercise normative authority? Arguably they generate normative reasons for action as long as they apply to agents who take themselves to be rational. Street assumes that humans are rational enough to make use of such requirements. But whence do such requirements derive their normative authority? On the Kantian view, the subjective normativity of such requirements is rooted in the agent's self-representation as the member of a community of rational beings; for some, these norms guide the agent in the activity of self-constitution. This answer, however, is not available in Street's theory since the appeal to self-representation plays no role in her theory. Thus, she needs to justify that the logical and instrumental requirements are normative and binding for all evaluators as such.

Despite these shortcomings, Street posits a fundamental question concerning the place of morality in our lives, removing constructivism from its original concern with moral obligations toward others. What is the source of moral authority? Why should the interests of others matter to any of us? Does morality oblige us to categorically respect the claims of others? These are questions that divide even Humean constructivists.

3.2 The Contingency of Moral Values

Divergences between the Kantian and Humean varieties of constructivism, such as Street's, concern the nature of rational norms that organize the activity of valuing and articulate how one should live as a valuer.[49] On the Kantian view, this question is addressed by representing oneself as a member of the universal

---

[48] Scanlon 2012, p. 231.

[49] "Is morality something we are bound to by the mere fact that we are valuers at all, or is our relationship with morality more contingent than that, though perhaps no less dear for that fact? I will be arguing for the latter view" (Street 2012, p. 42).

community of rational beings: Kant argues that respect for the capacity for self-legislation amounts to respect for others. A rendering of this view is that duties of respect identify the principles that could successfully coordinate a plurality of rational agents capable of setting their own ends in life (O'Neill 1996). According to Street, we should start with individual valuers who take practical standpoints with their particular baggage of values and beliefs. The dispute on the metaphysical commitments underpinning Kantian construction notwithstanding, Street's project is appealing because the wide diversity and natural history of moral customs and behavior demand an explanation, exerting pressure on universalistic ethics. In this regard, the purported advantage of the Humean strategy is that it vindicates the contingent aspects of morality. To assess the achievements of Humean constructivism, we should consider that coming to terms with contingency means acknowledging the radical diversity among individual evaluative starting points, so that "if one had entered the world with a radically different set of values, or were merely causal forces to effect a radical change in one's existing set of values, then one's normative reasons would have been, or would become, radically different in a corresponding way" (Street 2012, p. 42).

This position resembles metaethical relativism in that it renders practical reasons dependent on the set of values adopted by individual agents; therefore, practical reasons do not apply to all individual valuers as such, independent of the particular substantive values held by each one. Correspondingly, one cannot presume that immoralists take action without normative reasons, as it may seem based on Korsgaard's theory. Immoralists such as Caligula act immorally with reasons of their own, which follow from their particular sets of values (Gibbard 1999; Street 2009).

Street hastens to assuage worries about this form of relativism because it does not undercut the distinction between right and wrong. The moral variance allowed by Humean constructivism belongs within the bounds of reasons rooted in human nature. Within these bounds, nonetheless, rational agents find reasons to act that radically contradict one another and may even systematically undermine mutual prospects of a good life without ceasing to be reasons, as illustrated by the case of Caligula.

The advantages of Street's theory with regard to the vindication of contingency come at the cost of losing stable criteria to tell right from wrong, a loss that affects the nature of commitments to mutual intelligibility and cooperative interactions. On the Kantian view, cooperative interactions rely upon shared reasons, while Street believes that they depend on the contingent convergence of individual interests or preexisting moral feelings. The authority of all such reasons is local and conditioned on the hypothesis of such convergences:

> Moral feeling is something that an agent ultimately either has or does not have as part of his nature, and if an agent has no trace of it anywhere in his evaluative makeup, or if that feeling does not run deep enough when push comes to shove, then this is not a mistake in any genuine sense, on the Humean constructivist view; in that case, the agent simply is not, at bottom, a moral agent (Street 2012, p. 55).

The latter remark does not undermine Kantian constructivism, since Kantians might agree that the susceptibility to moral feeling is original and cannot be commanded; however, they would argue that it can be educated and developed, and to this extent, there is an obligation to develop moral sensibility (Kant Ak 6: 245; cf. section 1.2.4). The main point of disagreement concerns the powers attributed to practical reason and its role in the articulation of a good life.

Street is certainly correct in stating that the diversity of moral codes and costumes ought to be taken into account, in addition to their origins and relation to human nature. It can be said that *at least some* moral reasons have a broad scope and authority within a naturalistic framework and that their characteristic functions and features can be explained in relation to being human. Second, the advantages of Street's narrow definition of reason may also be queried from a naturalistic perspective. Practical reasoning as a problem-solving practice is arguably a tool that helps humankind to adapt, owing to the efficacy of principled reasoning in fostering agreement and coordination (Bagnoli 2019a). In this regard, Street's account of practical reason underestimates the pervasive role of reasoning and its central function in the organizational dynamics of social life. Exactly how does practical reasoning contribute to social life? How much variety is tolerable given the aim of achieving these contributions?

Whether a minimal or robust conception of practical reason is preferable partly depends on the prospects of accounting for the functions of practical reason without committing to an implausible metaphysical apparatus. Street's strategy avoids any awkward metaphysics; while this merit is not unique to her theory but shared with all antirealist theories, the critical question is whether it can sustain a plausible view of practical reasons and moral obligations. We shall revisit these issues in Section 4.

3.3 Categorical Practical Reasons and Moral Judgment

Street holds that categorical practical reasons may arise from values and concerns of contingent origins. Values come about contingently but generate categorical reasons. A recurring example is love: love for one's children is contingent, yet it generates reasons that are "categorical." The kind of categoricity that Street advocates for is such that whenever conflict arises, reasons borne out of love for one's children overrun other reasons for action. This is one distinctive understanding of categoricity, akin to "deliberative overridingness." This conception stands in contrast to Kant's categoricity, which is tightly related to universality, both in the scope of its application and its range of evaluators. The deliberative overridingness of practical reasons with respect to other considerations follows from and is explained by their lawlike form, which ensures the synchronic and diachronic coherence of categorical practical reasons, at least in principle. By contrast, the assertion that categorical reasons are local and particular cannot provide this assurance. There is no guarantee that categorical reasons thus understood would align with other reasons: the former may be incompatible with the latter, creating a rupture in the agent's practical standpoint that may eventually impede action.[50] The resulting view is a fragmented account of rational agency that is silent on why and how valuers should embark on the process of self-criticism and coherence-driven revision.[51]

As a general account of valuing, Street's theory may be found appealing precisely because it does not concur with Kantians about the centrality of morality. However, it raises concerns about the alleged function of *moral* judgment. According to Street, moral judgments convey and articulate individual evaluative attitudes as much as any other practical judgments. However, moral judgments play other, more complex social functions related to the recognition of one's place in the community. This feature can adopt different philosophical characterizations. For constructivists inspired by Kant and Hobbes, moral judgments favor cooperative interactions and support the enforceable duties and responsibilities of the participants in cooperative schemes (Gauthier 1986; Copp 2005; Brennan, Goodwin and Southwood 2013; O'Neill 2015). Other scholars underline the role of emotions such as shame in aligning individuals with the protection of societal shared goods and values (Gibbard 1990; Williams 1993). There is wide consensus that such functions are relevant to the way in which they exercise pressure toward conformity and compliance, at least regarding the observance of moral obligations (e.g., duties to respect for humanity), and also drive social criticism (Bagnoli 2019b; Thompson 2020). Different strains of metaethics may account for such pressure differently. The overarching point is that moral judgments fulfill social or coordinative functions because they are formulated

---

[50] Bratman 2012; Ridge 2012, pp. 154–55; cf. Mitchell-Yellin 2015. According to Smith (2013), a similar worry arises for standard Humean theories, and he suggests that the ideal agent also needs to have desires that induce coherence.

[51] It is a matter of contention whether the very domain of practical reasons is in itself fragmented. Some source of fragmentations may depend on the contrast between special obligations to particular others and general obligations to others. This contrast may run deep also in Kantian ethics.

from a stance that claims not only individual but also universal authority (at least with respect to the relevant moral community). Furthermore, this coordinative function of moral judgment also serves as a drive for dynamic interactions, which underpins phenomena of personal reform and societal transformation.[52]

These objections point to a weakness in the individualist perspective defended by Street, which may show a failure to generate coherence across time and across individuals and to justify normative changes and revisions. *If* these objections hold, they suggest that means-ends coherence may not be sufficient to govern human agency and allow for just coordination. This is a serious problem, but a remedy is in sight for supporters of the Humean approach.

3.4 The Appeal to Human Nature

In the next sections, I discuss some varieties of Humean constructivism that can compensate for the deficiencies of the individualist model of valuing outlined in the previous section. Despite his narrow conception of reason and its powers, Hume acknowledges that moral judgment is governed by general rules and that moral reasoning and moral judgment at least *aspire* toward objectivity and generality.[53] There are mechanisms that correct the individual stance and, at the same time, define the stance of moral judgment in terms of the general perspective. Such mechanisms, namely sympathy and general rules, are regulating devices that introduce objectivity into moral judgments, although doubts remain that an appeal to the general point of view does not erase all the possible biases rooted in the individual perspective.[54]

These resources help reorient the Humean constructivist agenda in a different direction. Recent advocates of Humean constructivism appeal to general rules and human nature so as to strengthen the explanatory capacity of constructivism (Lenman 2012; Driver 2017; Dorsey 2018). Such rules are contingent on the practical standpoint of social creatures, which builds and improves upon the

---

[52] In addition to views about ethical coordination for mutual benefits, some scholars convincingly argue that the distinctive function of moral norms and judgments consists in making it possible for the members of the moral community to hold one another accountable, see Brennan, Goodin, and Southwood 2013.

[53] Hume 2007, p. 585. Recent scholarship in Humean studies emphasizes the social aspects of Hume's ethics, see Taylor 2015. Hume's treatment of justice in particular represents morality as a cooperative enterprise, Taylor 2015, p. 192.

[54] "Judging in sympathy with a person's narrow circle and according to general rules, we are able to reach agreement about her character. We all approve and disapprove of the same characteristics, and as a result we come to share an ideal of good character. Our concepts of the virtues and vices in this way arise from the general point of view" (Korsgaard 2008, p. 263, 2019).

individual stance by imposing general rules.[55] This theory makes room for moral failures, self-correction, and practices of social alignment. To this extent, it represents a decisive amelioration of Street's constructivism. Since it explains the pressure toward generality as a thoroughly *natural* phenomenon generated by those social aspects of "human nature,"[56] this Humean strategy also purports to offer a theoretical advantage over Kantian transcendental arguments. Nonetheless, there are some reasons to believe that such correctives are not completely satisfactory.

First, the Humean strategy requires an account of "human nature," which proves to be rather problematic. While an essentialist solution to the problem is unfit for the Humean metaphysical agenda, a reductivist account of human nature would undermine the aspiration to ethical objectivity. The appeal to human nature, therefore, must be *indeterminate*: "We might argue that it is a feature of human beings that, as they move through the world as social beings, they are guided by certain considerations, such as the consideration that the well-being of another provides one with at least some reason to act" (Driver 2017, p. 176).

Second, the generalizing strategies are not sufficient to ground a stable relation between morality and the self. The sense of humanity and sympathy does not contain the power to achieve this much, and those with differing levels of sympathy do not share in the practical reasons (Driver 2017, pp. 180–81), with the result evidenced in Sections 3.2 and 3.3. Humean constructivists tend to discount the depth and relevance of moral disagreement as well as the variance of practical reasons, but this is a crucial unresolved issue.

Finally, despite these important adjustments to account for the social significance of moral and practical reasoning, it is questionable whether these authors have truly improved upon Street's position. The problem is methodological: can the Humean approach to generality vindicate its normative significance?[57] This line of questioning arises through a diagnosis of moral disagreement, which implies moral failure or error. In such cases, how does the need for correction arise, and on what authority can the demand for correction be advanced? The Humean paradigm explains the pressure toward

---

[55] "On the view that I favor we appeal to features of human nature, such as our capacity to sympathetically engage with others, which underlie norms of concern for others. Thus, our reasons are derived from our attitudes but in a 'corrected' way" (Dorsey 2018, p. 585).

[56] "Humanity's evaluative nature, then, is understood to be an empirical, contingent fact about the way human beings really are in our world: as a species, and as a contingent matter, we share certain values" (Driver 2017, pp. 178–79; Dorsey 2018, p. 586).

[57] For a more extensive rendering of this objection, see Korsgaard 2008, pp. 278–79. For a more positive view of Hume's resources to account for normativity, based on artificial virtues, cf. Schafer 2018, 2019b.

generality as a (social or individual) psychological pressure, but this may be insufficient to account for why and how individual perspectives ought to be corrected. The Humean theory of moral judgment acknowledges the pressure for compliance and conformity, but it provides no answer to the above questions, which concern the normativity of general norms and corrective mechanisms.

One may conjure a naturalistic story about how general standards emerge in order to serve general interests and the need for correction, thereby providing a plausible account of the social function of normative standards;[58] but such conjectures do not fully account for the normative authority of the general standpoint, nor do they explain why individuals should join the general standpoint. At best, they give a partial answer that is limited to and conditioned on sharing the interests of the general standpoint.

Furthermore, positing a kind of *psychological necessity*, as Driver proposes,[59] does not explain the normativity of the commitment to moral norms. If moral norms bind as a matter of psychological necessity, they fail to be normative in any interesting sense. At most, they identify regular patterns of behavior.

In short, the Humean approach fails to address how social animals endowed with the relevant psychological capacities such as sympathy can become *committed to* norms of sympathy, or why they have good reasons to endorse the general point of view. Social animals appear to be "in the grip" of these norms by virtue of being embedded in social practices. A plausible diagnosis of this failure to explain the broad phenomenon of normative authority is that these theories do not recognize the role of self-consciousness in the mechanisms underlying the normativity of social practices.

3.5 A Humean Perfectionist Strategy

One path out of the impasse is to deepen the reliance on human nature. This is the perfectionist strategy in support of Humean constructivism adopted by Dale Dorsey: "This view holds that normativity is not constructed by each individual's valuing attitudes, but instead by humanity's evaluative nature, that is, when humanity's evaluative nature issues a verdict. As such, this view is not fully disconnected from the individual contingent attitudes of particular agents

---

[58] Driver 2017, pp. 177–80. "As social beings communicating with each other on moral matters we have a strong interest in being intelligible to each other" (Driver 2017, p. 180).

[59] "It may be that we can make this case by positing a kind of psychological necessity to this sort of normative commitment, one that is an essential part, or constitutive of, what we consider recognizably moral behavior" (Driver, 2017, p. 7).

but it accords ultimate normative authority to the scrutiny of humanity's evaluative nature" (Dorsey 2018, p. 585).

Dorsey's view is inspired by Hume's reflection on the standard of taste, and it exploits the generic Humean claim that "nature is the true judge."[60] The argument is built by analogy with aesthetic judgments, which not only rely on the contingent evaluative judgments of qualified observers but also invoke a *standard*, that is, a rule upon which to reconcile differences and base decisions. This analogy seeks to establish that immoralists and eccentrics make mistakes (Dorsey 2018, p. 590) because there is "a subset of reasons that can be said to count in favor of our actions even if we lack the relevant valuing attitudes" (Dorsey 2018, p. 578). This "common core" includes values such as prevention of harm, caring for children and sick individuals, and beneficence.

Like its Kantian counterpart, the perfectionist strain of Humean constructivism recognizes that at least some moral reasons apply to all, but it does not assert that moral obligations are directly grounded in rationality alone (Dorsey 2018, p. 591). When the immoralist makes a mistake, this is not due to a failure of coherence. Immoralists are better described as socially dysfunctional and self-defeating agents who compromise a shared sense and understanding of ourselves as "socially productive."[61] Correspondingly, Dorsey agrees with Kantians that Caligula and the racist do make moral mistakes. Their evaluative attitude toward others does not limit the universality of the reason to prevent harm and maleficence. On the contrary, it means that their particular valuing attitudes are non-authoritative. The moral failures of racists occur in terms of contingent features of humanity, without which "our social world would be essentially unrecognizable." A qualified agreement by those whose sentiments are "in a sound state" counts as "evidence that human nature issues a particular verdict in a given case" (Dorsey 2018, p. 585). Moral failures are those that fail to reflect "the true sentiments of human nature" in one's own sentimental reactions. If one fails to conform, one also fails the normative standard.

The kind of convergence that matters is not whatever follows from adopting the general point of view, nor is it warranted by relying solely on the constraints of valuing as such. Rather, it is the convergence that we should expect among individuals whose judgments matter the most because they are qualified judges: "We care only about the verdicts of those who have some acquaintance with the subject matter of the relevant judgement," that is, knowledge, information, or experience within the subject of their sentiment (Dorsey 2018, p. 587). This is a minimum requirement, which works as a correction of the individual stance

---

[60] Hume 1985, pp. 190, 226–49, 229–30, 230–31.
[61] Driver 2017, p. 180; Dorsey 2018, p. 580.

and does not exclude other more substantive constraints that aid us in distinguishing between sound and unsound ethical judgments.[62]

Dorsey does not find the perfectionist strategy to be in violation of the formal characterization of the practical standpoint.[63] However, his strategy appears to overcome the problems of Street's account at the cost of abandoning the original rationale of constructivism. The perfectionist strategy is generally associated with normative realism, as well as with the view that there are values and reasons rooted in our nature and hence prior to and independent of rational choice and practical reasoning. Kantian constructivism regarding practical reason is defined and defended in stark contrast to (epistemic and moral) perfectionism (Rawls 2000; Pollok 2017).[64] By distancing itself from perfectionism, Kantian constructivism emphasizes the rational capacities unique to human agents as opposed to infinite rational beings. For finite and embodied rational agents, validation is importantly public (O'Neill 1989). Instead of the discovery of truth, the appeal to public reason emphasizes the claims of responsibility for judgment in the first-person perspective.

Thus, the perfectionist strategy brings Humean constructivism closer to moral realism than other Kantian and Humean varieties of constructivism by presuming a subject matter that stands independent of and prior to the construction of the agent. The construction reflects what *actual practices* recommend: "one way to come to understand the purely formal characterization of the practical point of view is by the extent to which this account of the practical point of view reflects our normative practice, which seems clearly to accept a shared common core" (Dorsey 2018, p. 594 n. 62). This formulation is objectionable on three grounds: first, it raises the issue of circularity, since it presupposes a common core that ought to be the result of construction. Second, it relies on the converging force and quality of actual practices, which is highly disputable: convergence might be very hard to achieve, or it may be achieved because of factors irrelevant to validity; furthermore, the expectation of convergence rules out the prospect of divergent but equally valid moralities, the possibility of which should be allowed even if one has reasons for rejecting this on the basis of universalist aspirations.[65] Third, it raises more questions

---

[62] "I do not here reject other constraints on what it may mean for one's evaluative judgements to be in a 'sound state'; I only insist, broadly, on an acquaintance requirement" (Dorsey 2018, p. 587).

[63] Dorsey 2018, p. 594 n. 62. It is unclear how a purely formal characterization of the practical standpoint can be rendered in terms of shared substantive contents.

[64] For a critique of O'Neill's conception of practical reason as a purported alternative to perfectionism, see Besch 2011.

[65] Dorsey is overly optimistic about both the range and quality of convergence: "It would be quite surprising to discover that racist and prejudiced attitudes are the product of 'near-universal' agreement among those who have had experience with, have engaged with, or otherwise have

than it can answer regarding the kind of expertise required for moral acquaintance – specifically, it denies that all rational agents are similarly positioned in relation to practical knowledge. All these issues depend crucially and ultimately on a substantive account of the evaluative nature of humanity.

3.6 Humean Constructivism as a Hybrid Theory

Humean constructivism promises to vindicate the objectivity and authority of practical judgments within the bounds of human nature. This promise is best fulfilled by fully exploiting the social and rational features of humanity, yet it is a matter of contention whether these elements can offer us a full-fledged metaethics. James Lenman argues in favor of a hybrid theory that combines constructivism as a first-order theory of the moral justification of reasons with an expressivist semantics of ethical judgments. While it is labeled as Humean, it shares with Kantian constructivism a claim regarding the unifying role of reason in articulating rational agency as well as a normative procedure for the justification of moral reasons, which reflects normative ideals of equality and freedom. For Lenman, Humean constructivism is thus "a form of expressivism articulated in reason."

Unlike Street, Lenman seeks resources to disqualify immoralism, but his rejection of the immoralist case of torture for fun is captured in terms of a profound unwillingness "to accept as a set of moral norms governing the society where I live any such set that permits torture" (Lenman 2012, p. 223). Critically, the notion of unwillingness is understood in terms of a subspecies of desires constrained by codeliberation. Instead of appealing to human nature as other Humeans do, Lenman calls attention to the diachronic normative community of subsequent selves: "Without some degree of normative community between myself now and at earlier times, without a degree of diachronic normative stability between my deliberative reflective self now and at earlier times, I doubt that normative thinking, as opposed to a much simpler kind of practical thought [...] would get off the ground" (2012, p. 221). Lenman thereby stipulates the necessity of a weak norm for the unification of agency: "in order then to be in the game of normative thought at all, I need to be in the business of seeking to unify my agency."[66] The need for unification is alive in practical deliberation, because this impels the ranking of conflicting desires so as to take action. However, the unification principle does not commit to any essentialist view of the self: "The unity of agency required to count as a maker of normative judgments at all is fantastically modest" (Lenman 2012, p. 221).

---

knowledge of the relevant 'outsiders'. Indeed, we have every reason to believe exactly the opposite" (2018, p. 597).

[66] Lenman 2012, p. 222; see also p. 221.

For Lenman, the most serious challenge faced by expressivism – adequately explaining objectivity as a feature of moral discourse – can be met by defending constructivism. But constructivism solves the metaethical problem regarding the nature of ethical objectivity through substantive normative means, and it does not qualify as a metaethical theory in itself. Moral constructivism therefore stands in need of a congruent metaethics that could substantiate its distinctive normative claims – a role which can be fulfilled by a well-established expressivist tradition.[67] The promised advantages of expressivism are the same as those of constructivism, since the vindication of objectivity comes at no cost in terms of ontology, and its account of the practical significance of ethical judgments avoids the problems of reductivist naturalistic analyses (Lenman 2012, pp. 217–18).

It is a matter of much debate whether expressivism can indeed vindicate the basic metaethical claims of constructivism regarding objectivity and practical significance. Korsgaard's reluctance to adopt the expressivist analysis arises from the conviction that it is unfit to characterize authority *in the first-person perspective* (Korsgaard 1996a); her more general point is that the relevant features of moral judgments cannot be captured by a semantic analysis of moral language and discourse. Furthermore, as Street points out, constructivism subsists on the distinction between valuing and desiring, which may be lost in the expressivist analysis of value. To be sure, expressivism needs to determine where desires stand in relation to reasons, and it may not be sufficient merely to label reasons as a subset of desires (cf. Lenman 2012, p. 221).

The critical question is what kinds of states that desires are and the kinds of functions that they are supposed to perform in the explanation of normative guidance.[68] Until these questions are adequately answered, no real progress can be made. Thomas Scanlon best formulates the dilemma that threatens to undermine this program: desire is either an overloaded evaluative term or a psychological one (Scanlon 1998, pp. 7–8, chapter 1). In the former case, no progress can be made by regarding reasons as species of desires. In the latter, the normative term is reduced to a psychological term in a way that fatally undermines the defining task of constructivism concerning normativity.

Although these issues remain largely unresolved, we can nonetheless draw some conclusions. First, expressivism (as a theory providing the semantics of ethical judgments) cannot serve as a mere completion of constructivism

---

[67] Gibbard 1990; Lenman 2012. On the relation between expressivism and constructivism, see Schafer 2014.

[68] A more promising semantics for a constructivist agenda builds upon Gibbard's research program, which does not rest on a mechanism of projection and captures dimensions and aspects of normativity central to the constructivist project.

(understood as a theory of the moral justification of reasons). This is because and insofar as these two theories construe the practical significance of ethical judgments differently, and thus they also differently conceive of the relation between semantics and moral justification. While expressivism focuses on how action can be driven by conative states, constructivism understands the practical significance of ethical judgments in terms of rational guidance by norms.

Second, Humean constructivism, understood as a variety of expressivism, views the role of construction to be very much akin to that of projection, along with Simon Blackburn's quasi-realism and his attempt to justify how antirealism can earn the right to truth.[69] The vindication of ethical objectivity is placed within an expressivist semantics, according to which

> the solidification into judgements imposed by normative discipline can be understood in terms of ways in which the applicability of norms of stability, of commonality, of coherence and consistency to what are, in the first analysis, passions in our souls, end up, if the quasi-realist project in metaethics can be made to succeed, intelligibly construed also, in the final analysis, as truth-apt judgments capable of at least some forms of objectivity
>
> (Lenman 2012, p. 220).

Entitlement to truth therefore rests on processes of "objectification" that depend on norms of rational choice. This explication of objectivity fulfills the requisite of "transparency" (Korsgaard 1996a, p. 17, section 2.1), unlike other projectivist accounts. This account takes the values of stability and commonality for granted, or at least borrows their explication from the agenda of Kantian constructivism. In the former case, it raises the worry of reification, which will be presented in Section 4.3.3; in the latter, expressivism is found parasitic on constructivism, rather than providing its completion; and the claim that constructivism requires expressivism remains ungrounded.

Third, constructivists and expressivists agree that "correct reasoning" is not correct because it tracks truths that emerge prior to and independently of such procedures. They also concur on the primacy of the practical and social task. Lenman also shares Korsgaard's view that constructivism rules out moral epistemology in any "genuine" sense, which is meant to imply that a genuine epistemology can be vindicated only from within a representationalist and realist theory. Once we forgo the realist claim that normative truths are prior to and independent of evaluators and their reasoning or valuing capacities, any interesting epistemological agenda is dissolved. Indeed, rational agents are not in the business of tracking truth while constructing their moral justification for

---

[69] Cf. Blackburn 1988. For the differences in the metaphors of vision, projection, and construction, see Bagnoli (2002).

action. For a constructivist, the problem of qualifying as objective judges and rational agents is not akin to "getting things right" in a way that assumes robust realism. Nonetheless, the question of knowing right from wrong extends beyond a matter of simply following the procedure of a given normative practice. This is where a distinct sense of practical knowledge becomes prominent, a sense which directly relates to rational agency. Constructivists therefore appear to adopt different conceptions of normative guidance. For some, the practical task is defined in opposition to the cognitive one. For others, however, practical knowledge is tied to authority of the first-person standpoint – and this is a variety of self-knowledge that makes moral epistemology crucial to some strains of constructivism regarding practical reason (Bagnoli 2013; Engstrom 2013). From this perspective, it is misleading to assume that epistemology rests on representationalism and robust realism. If we reject that assumption, constructivism's major advantage over rivals is precisely its epistemology: it provides an account of how practical knowledge is obtained, procedurally or by taking up a coherent moral stance or whatever, while the realists leave us with nothing better than intuitions into a dubious independent moral realm.

3.7 Conclusion

In this section, we considered different constructivist proposals to make room for contingency in accounting for the authority and objectivity of practical and moral reasons. By the Humean picture, the expectation of moral convergence produced by enjoying the general viewpoint is contingent on many factors external to rational agency. Some Humean constructivists lean toward relativism, maintaining that the recognition of contingency undermines aspirations for objectivity for practical reasons. Other varieties of Humean constructivism reject relativism with respect to practical reasons by embracing the notion of a set of core values general enough to be shared among all human beings by virtue of their human nature.[70]

In spite of the dissatisfaction of Humean constructivists with the Kantian account of the constitutive norms of rationality, it remains an open question as to whether and why the latter is found as problematic as robust varieties of realism since it entails no special moral ontology and allows for moral determinations as the result of practical reasoning. It may be impossible to avoid doing some metaphysics with respect to these issues (Korsgaard 2009; Schafer 2019a;

---

[70] Relativism can take many forms, not all of which are subjectivist. Moderate forms of relativism merely deny that there is a unique set of moral rules that is superior to all others. It can still maintain that context can determine which set is valid for an agent.

Thompson 2020), but this is not to say that constructivism falls back onto objectionable forms of moral realism. The metaphysics at work in Kantian constitutivism is not a theory of objects, but of the laws that govern and constitute reasoning and rational agency; in Kant's sense, these are laws *of* the subject, though not certainly decided by the subject (see O'Neill 1975, 1989; Watkins 2019).

Again, there is room for disagreement about what these laws command, and in particular whether the requirement of universality achieves anything more than logical consistency. Street believes that constructivism cannot support a noninstrumental account of practical reasoning, unless renouncing its formal method. The "normative essentialist" may reply that it is a matter of logical coherence to treat humans with respect, because it is a truth about humans that they are capable of giving themselves ends; and treating them differently is like denying this truth, committing a failure akin to logical contradiction (Guyer 2017, pp. 49, 65, viii, 144). For the constructivist, instead, immoralists who do not treat humans as capable of choosing are incoherent, but the incoherence arises between the rational principle of action and the judgment that these agents adopt in any particular case. The rational principle has the form of a law, not because there are normative essences to be respected, but because a principle can be normative, binding, or authoritative from the rational point of view only if it can be accepted as a law by the community of all rational beings; otherwise, it will be a principle with local authority, binding in a conditional way, depending on shared interests or purposes.

Lenman forcefully argues that immoral conduct such as torturing for fun is not borne out of moral ignorance, nor is it a "reflective" defect; it is more akin to a "distinctively political catastrophe, where our urgent aim of arriving at a shared set of moral understandings we are all willing to live with has failed" (Lenman 2012, p. 223). To fully capture this point requires us to switch from the question of what constitutes rationality or humanity to how the boundaries of the moral community are negotiated. This is the topic of the next section.

4 Practices of Rational Deliberation

The Kantian project of grounding morality in the constitutive norms of practical rationality assumes that the authority of such norms is beyond question. This position, however, is contestable. First of all, the constitutive nature of such norms can be understood in different ways: are they regulative ideals or effective binders of human agents? Second, if such norms bind with necessity, how can we assess the impact of contingences and make room for the autonomy of practical judgment?

For Kant, the norms of rationality necessarily apply to all rational beings, and rational necessity is warranted by lawfulness. This explains why the very activity of reasoning entails the capacity to legislate with oneself and others. Neo-Kantians regard practical necessity as inescapable, whereas Neo-Humeans deny that structural norms of practical reason could justify substantive moral obligations because such norms are formal, instrumental, and indeterminate. So-called reasons fundamentalists such as Thomas Scanlon deny their sufficiency in sustaining moral obligations (2003); others hold that the norms of rationality lack authority, and there are no grounds for sustaining a belief in practical reasons that comply with the requirements of rationality (Broome 2005).

An alternative approach to this issue is to refocus on the practices of deliberation. This section presents constructivist theories designed to accommodate the moral relevance of contingency by developing an account of the public and dynamic features of practical reason. To this end, they uncover the various roles of abstract universality, which they understand as concretely determinable and actualized in reality. These theories in turn provide different conceptions of the authority and objectivity of practical reasons, highlighting the variable scope of universal principles, which represent different shapes of humanity.

4.1 The Need for Abstract Principles

Unlike the Humean constructivists, O'Neill does not credit human nature with providing enough for spontaneous coordination,[71] nor does she trust mere convention as a source of authoritative principles. While she maintains that the ultimate basis for authoritative principles is reason, she does not recognize any "transcendent authority" in human reason.[72] O'Neill's constructivism is inspired by Kant's claim that reason possesses unconditional authority because and insofar as it is self-vindicating and addressed to an audience. She proposes a version of Kantian constructivism that appeals to the need for authoritative principles that allow for interdependent and mutually vulnerable finite rational beings to coordinate with one another.

The starting point of her argument is the "conditions of practical reasoning," in which a multitude of finite agents, mutually dependent in various ways and potentially engaging in interaction, search for principles to live by (O'Neill 1989, p. 213, 1996, p. 52). Under such circumstances, the problem of justice

---

[71] "No master plan is inscribed in each one of us; rather we must devise a plan. [. . .] This plan must not presuppose unavailable capacities to coordinate, such as a preestablished harmony between reasoners" (O'Neill 1989, p. 19).

[72] "There is no lofty position above the debate, as perhaps there might be if human reason had a transcendent source" (O'Neill 1989, pp. 46–47).

arises, and the only principles fit to solve such a problem are universal in scope: "principles that cannot be acted on by all must be rejected by any plurality for whom the problem of justice arises" (O'Neill 1989, p. 215).[73] While O'Neill holds that principles are always and necessarily abstract and indeterminate, she also clarifies that they do not constitute the full extent of practical reasoning: "They must always be applied in ways that take account of actual context; and they never determine their own applications" (1989, p. 216; cf. Lebar 2013, p. 193). The plurality of admissible principles which are mutually constraining limits the domain of their determinants, but the exercise of practical judgment is a requisite for an agent to determine the course of action in any given scenario.

O'Neill aims to establish the formal requirement of universality for the principles of coordination on practical grounds by showing that such a requirement allows for efficacy because it grants unconditional normative authority and respects all individuals as having equal normative standing. While coordination may be achieved via subordination, force, and social power, it would then fail to treat all individuals equally with regard to their normative standing.

O'Neill's argument builds upon Kant's conception of public reason (1989, chapters 1–2, 1996, chapter 2). The form of the test for rational justification is "modal," signifying that its authority does not rest on any hypothetical agreement, in contrast to contractualist forms of constructivism (Rawls 1971; Scanlon 1998; Hill 2001). O'Neill is critical of contractualist forms of Kantian constructivism because they are bound to select principles whose force and authority are conditional upon such an agreement. She is also critical of those varieties of constructivism that identify the constructive principles of reasoning with mechanisms of personal autonomy, such as reflective endorsement, because they cannot warrant unconditional authority (cf. Hill 1994).

In contrast to these prominent varieties of moral constructivism, she turns to and develops Kant's forensic metaphors of public reason alongside the metaphor of construction.[74] In contexts of discord and variance among a multitude of agents capable of setting on their own ends, any appeal to parochial authority would fail to provide the basis for agreement and coordination. Parochial reasoning rests on special sources of authorities such as officials in positions of powers, a church, or a syndicate. It appeals to a restricted audience and produces normative reasons that are authoritative and binding for a narrow set of agents. Such reasons have limited applicability, because they bind on the

---

[73] See also O'Neill 1989, pp. 210–15, 212, 1996, pp. 52, 48.

[74] O'Neill 1989, pp. 48, 70–71, 206, 2015, p. 32; cf. Street 2008a, p. 223. Contrary to Street's view, the test of universality does not check for internal coherence of the individual practical viewpoint, but seeks a public vindication of universal principles.

condition that the audience understands and accepts the interests and goals identified by any such special authority.

By contrast, the public use of reason derives its authority from the normative standards implicit or internal to public discourse: "what makes agreement of a certain sort authoritative is that it is agreement based on principles that meet their own criticism" (O'Neill 1996, p. 38).[75] In so doing, it designs an agenda that is agreeable and powerful enough to coordinate a plurality of individuals who recognize one another's equal normative standing but are driven by different interests and conceptions of the good life. This sort of coordination invokes normative principles of self-government, which rely neither on external authorities nor on mere actual agreement. The principles internal to reason are reflexive, lawlike, and negative in that they ensure the exclusion of self-serving and self-defeating principles. Crucially, the specificatin of their contents emerges through free and critical debates, which constitute the public use of reason in a concrete manner.

Although critics doubt that the recursiveness of reason would be sufficient to establish its unconditional authority (Watkins and Fitzpatrick 2002, p. 355), the reflexivity typical of the activity of reason is not equivalent to the recursiveness of a linear thought or algorithm.[76] Reasoning is not equivalent to a proof that something is true, but it aims at constraining an audience (O'Neill 2015, p. 46; Bagnoli 2021). In fact, practical reasoning may address different audiences, and the scope of its authority may vary accordingly. Public discourse targets a universal audience, and the scope sought in the construction of principles is universal. In this case, the constructed principles bind with unconditional authority.

The normative expectation of mutual respect and recognition of equal normative standing is grounded and explicated in terms of commitments that agents contract by taking action: "the conclusions about the scope of ethical consideration are derived from the assumptions to which agents commit themselves in acting" (O'Neill 1996, p. 110; cf. Arruda 2016). The conception of relevant individuals as free and equal rational agents is not constructed, but it is derivable from the bare description of the coordination problem alone.

Since the critique of reason is a continuous and reflexive process, an attempt at self-vindication exhibits a dynamic and a history. Analogous to a free public

---

[75] O'Neill 1996, p. 35. Public reason is the model of political discourse, and not vice versa (vs. Watkins and Fitzpatrick 2002).

[76] Critics of the recursive features of reason take the term to imply linearity, as in a simple algorithm. But the term "recursive" can be understood as iterative and linear, or dynamic. Reflexive does not mean linear or iterative.

debate, the possibility of making progress rests upon the development of practices of tolerance and mutual recognition (O'Neill 1996, p. 174). The law-like nature of the principles promises neither absoluteness nor eternal moral truths; instead, it allows for a flexible framework within which to organize personal communication. The activity of practical reasoning is thus understood to be productive and generative insofar as it depends on the dynamics of communication for its results. The realizability of mutual recognition requires that agents understand their intentions as dependent on others for their satisfaction. To this extent, O'Neill implicitly treats the relations of recognition as instances of collective intentionality.

This variety of constructivism emphasizes that the structural norms of rationality provide an incomplete account of the workings of practical reason, and thus it insists on the concrete dynamics of practical reasoning. An underappreciated merit of this approach is that it draws attention to moral improvement as a metaethical issue (Arruda 2017). Even though critics doubt that such a theory can provide a full-fledged and self-standing account of practical reasoning (Besch 2008, 2011; Barry 2013; cf. Ronzoni 2010), O'Neill's seminal work has nonetheless been a springboard for the ambitious varieties of constructivism about practical reason that abandon idealization and transcendental arguments in favor of concreteness.

4.2 Constructivism through Practical Wisdom

Aristotelian constructivism and O'Neill's notion of practical reasoning share a common ambition to provide a general account of the nature of practical truths as constructed rather than recognized (Cullity and Gaut 1997, p. 183). They also share the diagnosis that abstract principles of practical reason are indeterminate, and thus a theory of practical reasoning should account for the *exercise* of rational powers and practical judgment in context. Mark Lebar argues that the metaphor of construction may well capture the virtuous exercise of rational agency. A common thesis in ancient eudaimonism is that the value of all objects is conditional on the exercise of rational agency, which is the basic source of value (Aristotle NE III.4: 1113a32; EE VII.15:1249a10-12; NE V.1:1129b2-6). Goodness is constructed by correctly exercising practical rationality, that is, practical wisdom (*phronesis*). Practical reasons for taking particular actions or realizing particular aims cannot be adequately accounted for as ways of recognizing or responding to independently normative properties of the chosen ends of our actions; rather, the goodness of such ends is conditional upon their contribution to a good human life, and their contents are determined by practical reasoning.

A distinctive aspect of the Aristotelian conception of practical wisdom is that it is developed through practice and education, and requires habituation. The main task of moral habituation is not to rechannel or eradicate one's natural drives but for the novice to become reflective and self-consciously aware of the mechanisms of these impulses. Through practice and correct reasoning, one gains an appreciation not only for the springs of action but also for their rational credentials. Rather than silencing natural incentives in favor of an ideal of practical rationality, moral education reshapes emotions into a "second nature," so that the good human life is essentially both animal and rational (cf. McDowell 1995, p. 170). Thus, in contrast to the idealized models of rational agency and mechanism of reflective endorsement, the Aristotelian approach emphasizes the lasting transformative effects of moral education. Exercising rational capacities in the right way not only checks and orders current motives but also transforms natural dispositions into stable traits of character (Lebar 2008). To the extent that the emergence of moral character becomes second nature, it is traceable via psychological and social processes of moralization, and constructivism can be aligned with ethical naturalism. Moreover, this is a non-reductive form of naturalism that does not discount the operative effects of practical reason. This approach situates morality within a general account of practical wisdom as contributing to human flourishing (Aristotle NE 1103a 11-b20). While moral cognitions are the object of practical reason, the latter is *incomplete*: to be endowed with rational and emotional capacities is insufficient for grasping and articulating true moral cognitions. Such capacities ought to be adequately exercised and appropriately taught in order to generate genuine moral knowledge. The model emphasizes the role of dependence and reliance on social practices in developing and perfecting our natural endowments.[77]

This constructivist conception of practical wisdom leads to one of moral agency and the self: "We exist by virtue of activity (i.e. by living and acting), and [...] the handiwork [*ergon*] *is* in a sense, the producer in activity; he loves his handiwork, therefore, because he loves existence. And this is rooted in the nature of things, for what he is in potentiality, his handiwork manifests in activity" (Aristotle NE IX.7; cf. Lebar 2005). "Perception" (*aesthesis*) plays a role in practical judgment, but this role is captured through contrast with the model of the sensory perception of external objects (Aristotle NE

---

[77] Other interpretations emphasize moral cognition as a cognitive achievement which we gain over time by sharing a practice *under the exemplary guidance of the wise*, analogous to a craft (Aristotle NE 1141a 20- 1141b 8). In this case, the view invites an exemplarist epistemology that denies equality in the normative and moral statuses of all individual agents. The epistemo-logical role of the wise is an issue of Aristotelian ethics which warrants further investigation (cf. Bagnoli 2020).

VI.8,1142a30). In the practical case, perception is a matter of activity, and it represents the complex ways in which moral agents come to appreciate the patterns constitutive of living well by the reflective work of practical wisdom, which results from habituation. When the processes of habituation and moral education are completed and practical reason is fully formed, the exercise of practical rationality becomes *akin* to detecting or responding to the descriptive features of the world that warrant and demand action. Practical rationality rests on perception, but in a way that entails complex social processes of construction. In contrast to recognitional conceptions of practical reason, Aristotelian constructivism posits no facts about living well as a human being apart from the wise judgments of human agents on this issue. By extension, the canons for success in practical rationality are thought to be *themselves* objects of construction. This is because practical wisdom (*phronesis*) is just practical rationality exercised such that one lives well. Thus, the standard of success in practical rationality is not a formal criterion but a substantive one, shaped by living according to reason.

Aristotelian constructivism rejects any formal procedure or codification governing the work of practical reason; thus, it may be confused with a recognitional account of the function of reason, which commits to moral realism (Gaut 1997, pp. 177–78, 163). While the dichotomy between recognitional and proceduralist models of practical reason may shed some light on what is at stake in the post-Kantian debate about ethical formalism and the a priori laws of reasoning, it is less perspicuous for other theories of practical rationality. In the post-Kantian debate, constructivists and realists quarrel about the nature of the stopping point in the regress to the unconditioned as well as about the starting points of practical reasoning. Instead, Aristotelian constructivism maintains that practical judgments about what one ought to do are true as long as they guide the agents' activity toward living a good life.[78] What constitutes the good life is the result of construction, as are the criteria for success in life. Thus, a successful exercise of practical rationality – that is, leading to a good life – involves both successful reasoning (in the sense of identifying the proper inferential relations among beliefs and other attitudes) and making substantively correct choices regarding the best approach to living.

The Aristotelian model of practical reason may seem vulnerable to objections similar to the Euthyphro dilemma.[79] One way to raise this issue is to query the

---

[78] While Lebar (2008) does not deny that there are procedural constraints on practical reasoning, he believes that they are insufficient; Lebar (2013) argues from constructivism to particularism, in which moral principles lack epistemic significance.

[79] This sort of objection arises in particular for the Aristotelian models that invoke the role of the wise in determining the correct standard of practical reason. Insofar as the wise are accorded

nature of the constraints on construction: If they are not moral, then the construction faces the problem of indeterminacy among the principles constructed, and the question arises as to whether such principles are recognizable as a set of moral principles (Shafer-Landau 2003). If they are moral, then the approach is not thoroughly constructivist, since there are moral principles at work prior to construction, and it leads to the relativistic conclusion that different sets of moral assumptions yield divergent constructed outputs (Timmons 2003). According to Lebar, worries about the nature of the constraints arise on the assumption of a foundationalist structure as the basis for the constructivist project; but the role of constraints in construction is not analogous to the starting points in a foundationalist approach. Furthermore, the concerns regarding indeterminacy can be silenced only by engaging in a detailed normative ethics.

Building upon the debate about the impossibility of codifying moral judgments, Lebar argues that such practical judgments are *constitutive* of what is required by successful practical rationality.[80] His point is that this constructivist justification warrants the kind of objectivity that is worth having in the practical domain, that is, an objectivity that recognizes the force and impact of contingencies.[81]

The Aristotelian social construction of the moral self comprises peculiar features designed to avert the risk of relativism that besieges other such conceptions. There are objective constraints on the form of habituation and practice that lead to a good life. What qualifies as a good life and the goodness of such a life itself depend on the exercise of our practical rationality. The criteria for evaluating the kinds of lives that can be regarded as successful are objective, although the good life is a construction which results from effectively exercising that very capacity for practical rationality.

On this view, practical rationality is regarded as not abstracted from but rather immanent in our animal natures. However, the constraints on construction are objective to the extent that practical reasons are "open to a public discipline" and not the expression of private interests or individual attitudes concerning the good life. Such a discipline imposes standards of correctness shared by all in

---

ultimate authority in establishing the standard of correctness for moral cognition, the model appears to be arbitrary and may not offer any measures against bias. On the other hand, if the wise do not mark the standard of practical knowledge, then their role is only heuristic, and thus this model is critically incomplete.

[80] "Excellence, then, is a state concerned with choice . . . this being determined by reason and in the way in which the man of practical wisdom would determine it" (NE II.6:1107a1-2).

[81] To this extent, Aristotelian constructivism sides with John McDowell's critique of objectivity understood as committing to an external and detached perspective on life, in which contingencies do not matter (McDowell 1979, p. 339, 1981, p. 155). Cf. Hursthouse 1987, pp. 247–59.

terms of leading a good life (*orthos logos*, NE VI.1: 1138b25). The exercising of practical rationality on this view warrants a form of agential autonomy that is only partly analogous to the agentive status conferred by Kantian constructivism to practical subjects (Lebar 2005).

The Aristotelian model contains profound insights into the incompleteness of practical reason and the social dimension of its completion, for example, the need to learn under the normative guidance of others, and the crucial importance of others in ordinary practices of self-governance and self-regulation. To this extent, it also raises important issues regarding the status of social emotions, and their positive contribution to personal autonomy. At the same time, this account raises worries regarding the place of individual self-determination as well as the foundation of moral equality of individuals and their status of authoritative sources of moral claims.[82]

A related and outstanding question concerns the epistemological role of moral principles, which also serve as principles of self-governance and self-determination in the Kantian view. Korsgaard (2019) engages with neo-Aristotelian accounts of constitutivism, and argues that they fail to make sense of moral responsibilities because they cannot sustain the claim that the self is responsible for its personal identity and its self-constitution.

4.3 The Historicity of Practical Reason

Some varieties of constructivism have developed O'Neill's thesis on the incompleteness of practical reason and the importance of communication, embracing the Hegelian tradition. The basic method and principles for justifying practical norms are rooted in Kant's constructivism, as explicated and defended by O'Neill.[83] While stressing their lineage to the Kantian critical project, Hegelian constructivists adapt and develop its core tenets in a way that deepens the contrast already emphasized by O'Neill between constructivism and contractualism.[84] The criterion for practical reason is modal rather than hypothetical; the relevant

---

[82] These worries do not necessarily arise for Lebar, but they need to be addressed, in contrast to exemplarist account of practical wisdom, which deny moral equality. Lebar adapts Aristotle's ethics in a way that does not implicate the reliance on the judgement of the wise and therefore does not seem to recommend an exemplarist conception of objectivity. It is disputable as to whether the operative mode of normative guidance by others is imitative or emulative, so the appeal to others may account for the attainment of practical knowledge aside from their roles as models or exemplars of virtue.

[83] Both Kantian and Hegelian constructivist theories highlight the progressive work of practical reason, although not in a way that reintroduces contractualist bargaining scenarios (see O'Neill 2003; Westphal 2016).

[84] There are different assessments of the continuity between Kantian and Hegelian constructivism (see Geldstill and Stein 2020). For the distinctive conception of actuality at the core of Hegelian constructivism, see Redding 2020.

facts are social rather than counterfactual; and the theory is objectivist – or at least it purports to construct norms with objective rather than subjective validity. But in contrast to the modality of possibility chosen by O'Neill, neo-Hegelians insist on the modality of *actuality*, which necessitates the development of reason through its concreteness while making room for alternative (and even thwarted) possibilities (Ng 2009; Yeomans 2012; Redding 2020). The result is a powerful account of practical reason that hopes to vindicate the historicity of practical reason and offer a complex, multi-dimensional social exploration of individual autonomy. The constraints at work in practical cognition are themselves social and answerable to the constructed norms of a community of rational agents at any given sociohistorical moment. Rational agency is not an exclusive matter of the self-relation and self-determination of an individual; instead, it requires appropriate engagement with and recognition by others.

While all the constructivist models inspired by Hegel's social philosophy advocate for the ontological, epistemic, and ethical priority of social processes over the individual exercise of rational agency, they disagree about how to conceive of this priority. As a result, they occupy distinct positions in the debate over realism. The differences parallel exegetical disputes over the distinctive ontological commitments associated with the Hegelian claim that moral reality and normativity depend on the actual social and ethical order (*Sittlichkeit*). For some, this claim entails that moral normativity is "invented or made" rather than discovered (Pippin 2008, p. 75). Others resist the implication that moral reality and normativity are "invented" because human nature is already constantly shaped by the ethical order (Laitinen 2020; Thompson 2020). Since the normative realm is social from the start, it is neither the result of any preexisting human agency nor created by concrete individual or collective acts. To vindicate this claim and stress the anti-relativist commitments, this second strand of Hegelian constructivism retains the term "realism" but in a qualified form, for example, as a *weakened* realism (Ostritsch 2020 subsection 7.3.3) or as a *realism mediated* by historical formations (Laitinen 2020). A third strand maintains that the core claim about the social nature of constructions is *neutral* – albeit markedly objectivist – regarding moral realism and its alternatives (Westphal 2016, pp. 17, 1, 3). Finally, others agree with Korsgaard that constructivism posits a challenge to the dichotomy between realism and skepticism (Wretzler 2020). Hence, different proposals have been put forth concerning the role and impact of social constructions.

4.3.1 Social Artifacts

According to social constructivism, normative truths are social artifacts. Social construction is at the root of the objectivity and authority of practical reasons.

While Hegelian constructivism commits to the objectivity and universal normativity advocated by Kantian constructivism, it faces different challenges regarding the nature of social construction. The novelty of this variety of constructivism is best elucidated in contrast to Kantian constructivism; it builds upon a critique of the attempt to derive duties from the absence of contradiction, which is considered nothing but an abstract indeterminacy (Hegel 1991, §135). Conversely, Hegelian constructivism *prioritizes* the social structure over individual rational will, thus it requires a different means of accounting for agential autonomy compared to previous models. In its most radical form, it claims that autonomous individuals must not simply be "assumed" to be irreducible agential stances, but they should be embedded in a sociopolitical reality (*Geist*). This claim commits to an investigation of the ontological features of such reality, which is an agenda in social ontology.

Social constructivists insist that self-determination and individual choice are possible only within social reality, and they suggest modulating the authority and objectivity of practical reasons across different social formations and concrete determinations. To this extent, constructivism is a program within the theory of social agency that calls attention to the multiple dimensions of individual autonomy, understood as forms of life lived by human beings, as belonging to a system of political and social institutions. Sociopolitical normativity requires the recognition of individual self-determination as well as of the communal dimension.[85] Recognition of oneself as a member of the relevant community is obtained through education (*Buildung*), a core feature of the complex processes through which normativity is produced. Norms express irreducible individual and collective freedoms, and content is provided by the concrete determinations to which these individuals and collectives freely commit. Hegelian constructivism shares the Kantian ideal of moral equality, but its purported comparative advantage is that it explains how it becomes realized and effectual by refocusing on the social and temporal dynamics of rational agency and uncovering its social and historical embedding. Yet this variety of constructivism is hardly distinguishable from relativism unless history is granted an inherent rationality.[86]

4.3.2 Construction as Sublation

To avoid relativistic consequences while capturing the role of concrete and historical embedding, Arto Latinen (2020) conceives of construction in terms of

---

[85] In contrast to the emphasis on individual choice, see Moyar 2011, pp. 68ff.

[86] As an alternative to both these options, the socialized view of Kantian constructivism distinguishes "practical reason as such," which is empty, from its concrete realization, see Walden 2012, 2018.

the Hegelian concept of sublation (*Aufhebung*), which names a dialectical process of conservation and change. Sublated constructivism holds that while social constructions are structurally required and epistemically relevant, they do not constitute the ultimate normative criteria of practical judgments. Rather, they form the concrete guidelines that enable individuals to make rational choices from within their social realities. Social constructions have structural, epistemic, and contextual normative functions, all of which codetermine the contents of practical truths. The concrete social form of life (*Sittlichkeit*) also serves as a repository of past collective commitments that shape the normative landscape.[87] This is one major means through which established ethical practices fulfill their normative function, especially regarding how they infuse collective and individual identities.

An important merit of this model is that it accounts for the fallibility of moral agents as well as of the concrete social formations in which they live, and it does so in ways that are not reducible to the defects of individual rational willing. Objectively good contents may not be accessible to the participants in a form of life; alternatively, their normative relevance to practical truths may be obscured, restricted, or filtered out. Thus, reliance on social constructions does not entail that social practices are invulnerable to internal critique or self-correction.

Within this fallibilist framework, sublated constructivism appreciates the epistemic and normative relevance of feelings of suffering. The role of moral sensibility is therefore not confined to an account of moral motivation; rather, it assumes the larger normative and epistemic function of detecting and responding to wrongs, serving as means of political and ethical empowerment. The epistemology of sublated constructivism is characterized by trial and error: individual agents acknowledge specific shortcomings of the historical reality by living within it, adhering to the norms and conceptions of the good distinctive of it.

By focusing on concrete ethical formations, this variety of constructivism draws attention to the respective distributive prospects for the division of labor and of responsibility as well as to their temporal patterns. Therefore, it promises to account for "historical" modes of alienation that elude the mechanisms of reflective endorsement due to their roots in specific sociohistorical conformations.

4.3.3 The Metaphysics of Actuality

The main challenge to Hegelian constructivism lies in characterizing the metaphysics appropriate to support the historicity and normative significance of

---

[87] Yeomans highlights the connection between the abstractness of reason and historicity, which is more complex than entailed by the focus on temporal duration, or change, see Yeomans 2012, 2020.

practical truths. The view that ethical constructions are social artifacts leans toward antirealism, but it struggles to explain how the entitlement to truth can be earned. A social constructivism without any robust commitment to ontology is insufficient to vindicate these features, because it is exposed to two related but distinct objections: relativism and reification (Thompson 2020). On the one hand, by grounding reasons in sociohistorical contexts, social constructivism deprives them of their critical power, leading to relativism. On the other, there is a risk of reification, since practical reasons nested in shared norms and practices tend to be invulnerable to rational scrutiny.

For the qualified forms of realism, instead, the problem is both ontological and epistemological. On the former issue, a nodal point in current debates concerns the requirement of metaphysical parsimony, which has been largely taken for granted, but arguably at the expenses of a full understanding of normative phenomena.

Michael J. Thompson argues that constructivism goes astray in seeking to emancipate moral reasoning from any metaphysical assumptions. The Hegelian approach explicates the need for a social ontology by conceiving of "human beings as essentially social [. . .]; their social relations are the very substance of their social reality, shaped and reworked into different ontological forms through history" (cf. Redding 2020; Thompson 2020). The envisioned solution relies on a comprehensive metaphysical structure of reason that works through institutions and affirms the centrality of interdependent and embedded individuality. This theory still qualifies as constructivist to the extent that it affords a kind of objectivity *internal* to concrete social formations; unlike relativist forms of constructivism that are based on the contingency of conventions or intersubjective agreement, this theory stems from the ontological structures of social life. Its distinctive focus on actuality allows us to appreciate the dimension of reflective conscience, which is not merely an output of reflexivity but also manifests consciousness of the self as belonging in concrete ethical formations.

The weak spot is that rational agents are *relied upon* to think in terms of reasons that capture the systemic totality – that is, the actuality – of their social world. But on which grounds are they to be trusted? Whether this is a realistic expectation may depend on contextual features, and it is hard to understand how to differentiate the purported confidence to grasp the actuality of the social world from reification.

4.4 The Problem of Normative Revision

The theories examined in Sections 4.1–4.3 attempt to correct or overcome the infelicities of constructivism that depend on the idealization and abstraction of its method. While Hegelian constructivism refocuses on actuality, Aristotelian constructivism favors the disposal of universal principles in practical deliberation. This discussion requires us to rethink the role of universality in practical reasoning and to revisit current accounts of normative revision.

The metaphor of construction aptly captures the dynamic dimension of normativity as a means of normative change, insofar as it represents practical reasoning as opposed to proofs and deductive inferences. The recognition of the dynamic dimension of normativity bears disastrous consequences for deductivist accounts of practical reasoning, but where does it does lead us? For some it leads toward particularism.[88] This is because in the practice of rational justification, universal principles do not provide all the relevant information that one can apply to defuse all the possible defeaters. Unlike deductive inferences, universal principles in constructivism do not serve as the fixed starting points of practical reasoning, nor does the structural norm of universality suffice on its own to determine practical judgment.

While Kantian constructivists acknowledge that procedures and abstract principles do not constitute the full extent of practical deliberation, they have devised various strategies to account for normative revision. In recognition of the epistemic limitations of human agents, Korsgaard introduces a distinction between "merely universal principles" and "provisional principles."[89] The latter are not merely general: they commit rational agents to revision whenever they encounter an exception, whereas general principles are insensitive to exceptions. This distinction seems to suggest that moral principles take the form of "summary rules" in ordinary moral thinking since strictly universal principles are unavailable to human agents.[90] Ordinary agents make progress by revising the principle and "bringing it a little closer to the absolute universality to which provisional universality essentially aspires" (Korsgaard 2009, p. 74). Now construction resembles a piecemeal approximation of a regulative ideal as well as the trial and error epistemology advocated by Laitinen (2020).

Moral progress, however, is not a mere incremental adjustment, and it can be described in terms of a reasoned reorientation toward others, which is disruptive and demands self-transformation. To this extent, the epistemology for this task

---

[88] "The motivation for being constructivists should move us to be particularists as well" (Lebar 2013, p. 200). On the contrary view, see Bagnoli 2018.

[89] "There is no reason to suppose that we can think everything in advance. When we adopt a maxim as universal law, we know that there might be cases, cases we had not thought of, which would show us that it is not universal after all. In that case, we can allow for exceptions. But so long as the commitment to revise in the face of exceptions is in place, the maxim is not merely general. It is provisionally universal" (Korsgaard 2008, p. 123, 2009, pp. 74–75). For a critique, cf. Bagnoli 2018.

[90] On the contrast between principles as "summary rules" and the "practice" conception of principles, see Rawls 1955.

has to be both dialectical and dialogical (cf. Skorupski 2010, p. 29), unlike the epistemology of trial and error. The term "fallibility" is misleading if we want to remain true to constructivism and deny that normative truths represent a special domain of objects. Practical truths are not knowable through the ways in which the external (social) world impinges upon our minds; they are known by active and self-aware exercises of rational powers, including inferential capacities and normative dispositions and attitudes. But such powers are not exercised in a social vacuum, and there are strong reasons to believe that the extent and effectiveness of these exercises depend on social and contextual features.

4.5 Toward an Open-Ended Moral Community

Aristotelians and Hegelians argue that the appeal to abstract universality is insufficient to account for the dynamics of normativity. Borrowing from O'Neill, one may retort that the problem lies in idealization instead of in abstraction. Abstraction is inevitable and does not compromise rational justification. By contrast, idealization may fail to apply to the domain of choice, thus rendering it useless (O'Neill 1989, pp. 5–6); it is also potentially dangerous insofar as it covertly endorses enhanced versions of humanity, thereby excluding from the scope of relevance those who do not fi t into it. The moral of O'Neill's argument is that ideals of persons must be vindicated, that is, supported by reasons that *all relevant others* can share.[91] Only such reasons could warrant legitimate authority, as long as they are universal in scope.

In her critique of Rawls' contractarianism, O'Neill holds that idealization – understood as blanket ignorance of second-order desires – obscures the agents' own positions and "[deprives them of] reasons to care about the future beyond their own lives" (O'Neill 1989, p. 3). But contractarianism is said to be constructive because "it is a procedure that can settle disputes" (O'Neill 1989, p. 2), which implies that the main task of constructivism is to solve the practical problem of coordination via arbitration. This is certainly no minor task. In fact, Thomas Baldwin argues for universalization as the normative revision method of socially enforced moral principles, along with an allowance for appraising individual claims and correcting normative practices. The principle of reciprocity that binds agents of equal standing plays a crucial role in the procedure for handling complaints about existing practices, and it determines when the complaints are legitimate and should lead to reform and revisions (Baldwin

---

[91] Cf. Rawls 1989, pp. 514, 516. "The conceptions of society and person as ideas of reason are not, certainly, constructed any more than the [procedural] principles of practical reason are constructed" (Rawls 1993, p. 108; also pp. 104, 121–22). That these conceptions are not constructed does not mean that they are unjustified; they could be justified as congruent with ordinary moral thinking. This route leads us to the issues addressed by social constructivism.

2013, p. 219). This is an example of leveraging the appeal to universality to revise the content of socially enforced moral principles, but it is not the only way of making progress. In other cases, progress is made by introducing novel norms, which reduce the indeterminacy of moral problems.[92] Yet another major mode of making progress is by revisiting the scope of applicability of universal principles. O'Neill's point is that not all constructive norms are meant to foster coordination within a given community. Another way in which constructivism is of practical relevance is that it does not take any given community for granted. By avoiding idealizations, constructivism faces the issue: who are the relevant others? Or else, to whom to give voice?

Hegelians have insisted that to answer these questions, it is not enough to appeal to humanity as an unconstructed fact of nature or an absolute value beyond criticism. How should we negotiate the boundaries of novel normative communities? Understanding humanity and its boundaries is a matter of social recognition, and recognition is often the result of a struggle. But practical reasoning can also be recruited to the task of negotiating the boundaries of the moral community. In this manner, a constructivist metaethics rationally obliges us to take up the project of social transformation and social freedom. The challenge is to keep a meaningful reference to the moral community while making its boundaries open (Richardson 2018, p. 66). And, moreover, how is a moral community united?[93] These problems pertain to the project of under-standing how an open-ended society of all persons can be articulated so as to maintain an authoritative voice (Richardson 2018, p. 7).

The varieties of constructivism discussed in this section reject the view of practical reasons and normative truths as timeless and absolute, but do not abandon the view that there are rational criteria of their objectivity and norma-tive authority. A major point of dispute concerns the appeal to abstract universal principles as the structure of the construction, which seems insufficient to account for the social dynamics of normativity. The focus on such dynamics encourages us to rethink the role of universality in practical reasoning and its scope. Normative revisions and questions regarding the shape of humanity have thus become metaethical issues.

5 A Balancing Act

In 1992, the question was raised as to whether constructivism really qualifies as a metaethics (Darwall, Gibbard, and Railton 1992, p. 13). Some thirty years

---

[92] Stressing the temporal unfolding of the reflective equilibrium would lead to what Richardson calls "constructive ethical pragmatism" Richardson 2018, pp. 41, 48.

[93] This is one way the question shapes up: how can all persons be united by dyadic normative relations into a single moral community? cf. Richardson 2018, p. 118.

later, it is fair to say that constructivism has engaged its opponents in a sustained exchange about the nature of rational agency and the norms, scope, and impact of practical reason. While it is difficult to settle on a definitive chart that situates constructivism alongside other metaethical theories, its inclusion in the ongoing debate has undoubtedly shifted the focus of metaethics away from semantics narrowly conceived so as to take the nature of rational agency, moral psychology, and social ontology as factors that play important roles in determining meanings and their contextual dependencies.

The contribution of constructivism to metaethics has often been judged comparatively: with a scorekeeping model in terms of "plausibility points" aiming at a sort of "balance scorecard" (Shafer-Landau 2003; Enoch 2011; Southwood 2018), often implicitly accepting a tradeoff between normativity and objectivity (Smith 1994). Constructivism shares with naturalism the claim that normativity is enabled by certain distinctive mental capacities, that is, reflexivity. Like non-naturalism, however, it takes the putative autonomy of the normative very seriously, rejecting any reduction of normative truths in naturalistic terms. Unlike projectivism and error theory, constructivism shuns the conclusion that there are no non-trivial truths about normativity. In contrast to non-naturalism, moreover, it maintains that truths about normativity are explainable – they are more than mere brute and primitive items in a moral ontology. The varieties of constructivism covered in this study render these assertions partial or provisional.

Some of the objections raised against constructivism are formidable and concern – in particular – the versions of constructivism that aim to ground moral obligations in our identity as humans (Enoch 2006) or in structural norms of rationality (Scanlon 2012). The constructivist approach to the objectivity and authority of moral reasons stands in stark contrast to other views of the authority of morality. Many scholars agree that morality presents itself with ubiquitous and inescapable authority; but for others, an assumption of the inescapable authority of morality is merely question-begging (Copp 2015, p. 139). The matter is often assessed by considering conflicting cases of deliberation, in which moral reasons clash with reasons of self-interest. On Kantian and Hegelian perspectives, moral obligations derive their unconditional objectivity from the universality of the rational capacity, but whether this solves the problem also depends on the scope of rationality. On a narrow conception of rationality, the conflict between moral and self-interested reasons is a normative one, that is, a clash between the overall verdicts of differing normative standpoints. To call someone irrational is to charge him with a normative failure (Shafer-Landau 2003, p. 168; Parfit 2011, p. 56). Nonetheless, there are different conceptions of the rational standards. If rationality is understood solely in instrumental terms, then it becomes an open question as to which set of reasons will prevail in any given deliberative situation. For some, there is a strict connection between rationality and morality. For others, however, the question amounts to whether verdicts of morality are "more important" than those of self-interest. In this latter view, a failure to be morally motivated is not normatively significant in itself, because the only significant failures are those of rationality (Copp 2015, p. 139). Thus, there is not only a mismatch between rationality and morality, but also a controversy concerning the extension of their respective domains, and the requisites of rationality.

This essay attempted to illustrate the centrality of this dispute to metaethical inquiry. The main achievements of constructivism can be highlighted by focusing on construction as an activity undertaken by rational agents, either individual or socially bonded. Unlike other metaphors used in metaethics, construction brings to light the generative and dynamic dimension of practical reason. While they adopt various forms of abstraction and idealization, constructivists have formulated a profile of the relevant agents in charge of rational justification, one that is capable of accounting for the rational negotiation and articulation required to keep the moral community both united and open-ended. On the resultant picture, practical reasoning is not only productive but also self-transforming, and potentially socially empowering.

A promising new direction of research exploits the metaphor of construction even further, uncovering the social normative dynamics of rational deliberation beyond any settled moral community. Can such a metaphor be usefully extended to account for novel normative communities, including various animal, artificial, and hybrid collectives? These are the challenges that lie ahead.

References

Allison, Henry E. (2006). Kant's Transcendental Idealism. In Graham. Bird, ed., *Companion to Kant*. Oxford: Blackwell, pp. 111–24.

Ameriks, Karl. (2003). On Two Non-Realist Interpretations of Kant's Ethics. In Karl Ameriks, *Interpreting Kant's Critiques*. Oxford: Oxford University Press, pp. 263–82.

Archard, David, Monique Deveaux, Neil Manson, and Daniel Weinstock, eds. (2013). *Reading Onora O'Neill*. London: Routledge.

Aristotle (2000). *Nicomachean Ethics*, Oxford: Oxford University Press. [Abbreviated NE]

Arruda, Caroline T. (2016). What We Can Intend: Recognition and Collective Intentionality. *Southern Journal of Philosophy*, **54(1):** 5–26.

Arruda, Caroline T. (2017a). The Varieties of Moral Improvement, Or Why Metaethical Constructivism Must Explain Moral Progress. *Ethical Theory and Moral Practice*, **20(1):** 17–38.

Arruda, Caroline T. (2017b). Why Care About Being an Agent. *Australasian Journal of Philosophy*, **95(3):** 488–504.

Arruda, Caroline T. (2018). Why Moral Status Matters for Metaethics. *Journal of the American Philosophical Association*, **4(4):** 471–90.

Bagnoli, Carla. (2002). Moral Constructivism: A Phenomenological Argument. *Topoi*, **21:** 125–38.

Bagnoli, Carla. (2013). Constructivism About Practical Knowledge. In Bagnoli 2013, pp. 153–82.

Bagnoli, Carla. (2017a). Constructivism in Metaethics. In Edward N. Zalta, ed., *Stanford Encyclopedia of Philosophy*. https://plato.stanford.edu/archives/win2017/entries/constructivism-metaethics/.

Bagnoli, Carla. (2017b). Constructivism and the Moral Problem. *Philosophia*, **44(4):** 1229–46.

Bagnoli, Carla. (2017c). Kant in Metaethics: The Paradox of Autonomy, Solved by Publicity. In Matthew Altman, ed., *The Palgrave Kant Handbook/Palgrave Handbooks in German Idealism*. London: Palgrave Macmillan, pp. 355–77.

Bagnoli, Carla. (2018). Defeaters and Practical Knowledge. *Synthese*, **195(7):** 2855–75.

Bagnoli, Carla. (2019a). Ethical objectivity: The test of time. *Ratio* 32 (4):325-338.

Bagnoli, Carla. (2019b). Authority as a Contingency Plan. *Philosophical Explorations*, **22(2):** 130–45.

Bagnoli, Carla. (2021). The Practical Significance of the Categorical Imperative. *Oxford Studies in Normative Ethics*, **11**: 178–99.

Bagnoli, Carla, ed. (2013). *Constructivism in Ethics*. Cambridge: Cambridge University Press.

Baiasu, Sorin. (2016). Constitutivism and Transcendental Practical Philosophy: How to Pull the Baiasu, Sorin. (2020). Staying Philosophically on the Surface: Constitutivist and Naturalist Quests for Normativity. In *Reason, Normativity and Law: New Essays in Kantian Philosophy*. University of Wales Press

Rabbit Out of the Hat. *Philosophia*, **44(4)**: 1185–208.

Baldwin, Thomas. (2013). Constructive Complaints. In Bagnoli 2013, pp. 201–20.

Barry, Melissa. (2013). Constructivist Practical Reasoning and Objectivity. In Archard et al. 2013, pp. 17–36.

Besch, Thomas M. (2008). Constructing Practical Reason: O'Neill On the Grounds of Kantian Constructivism. *Journal of Value Inquiry*, **42(1)**: 55–76.

Besch, Thomas M. (2011). Kantian Constructivism, the Issue of Scope, And Perfectionism: O'Neill On Ethical Standing. *European Journal of Philosophy*, **19(1)**: 1–20.

Bird-Pollan, Stephan (2011). Some Normative Implications of Korsgaard's Theory of the Intersubjectivity of Reason. *Metaphilosophy*, **42(4)**: 376–80.

Blackburn, Simon. (1998). *Ruling Passions: A Theory of Practical Reasoning*. Oxford: Oxford University Press.

Bratman, Michael E. (1998). The Sources of Normativity. *Philosophy and Phenomenological Research*, **58(3)**: 699–709.

Bratman, Michael E. (2012). Constructivism, Agency, and the Problem of Alignment. In Lenman and Shemmer 2012.

Brennan, Geoffrey, Eriksson, Lina, Goodin, Robert E. and Southwood, Nicholas. (2013). *Explaining Norms*. New York: Oxford University Press.

Brink, David O. (1989). *Moral Realism and the Foundations of Ethics*. Cambridge: Cambridge University Press.

Brink, David O. (1992). A Puzzle about the Rational Authority of Morality. *Philosophical Perspectives* **6**:1-26.

Broome, John. (2005). Does Rationality Give Us Reasons? *Philosophical Issues*, **15**: 321–37.

Cholbi, Michael J. (1999). Egoism and the Publicity of Reason: A Reply to Korsgaard. *Social Theory and Practice*, **25(3)**: 491–517.

Cohen, Gerald A. (1996). Reason, Humanity, and the Moral Law. In Gerald A. Cohen, Raymond Geuss, Thomas Nagel, and Bernard Williams, eds., *The Sources of Normativity*. Cambridge University Press, pp. 167–88.

Cokelet, Bradford. (2008). Ideal Agency and the Possibility of Error. *Ethics*, **118(2):** 315–23.

Copp, David. (1995). *Morality, Normativity, and Society.* Oxford: Oxford University Press.

Copp, David. (2005). "A Skeptical Challenge to Moral Non-Naturalism and a Defense of Constructivist Naturalism", *Philosophical Studies*, **126(2):** 269–283.

Copp, David. (2008). Darwinian Skepticism About Moral Realism. *Philosophical Issues*, **18(1):** 186–206.

Copp, David (2015). Rationality and Moral Authority. *Oxford Studies in Metaethics* **10**: 134-159

Cullity, Garrett and Berys Gaut eds., 1997, *Ethics and Practical Reason*, Oxford: Clarendon Press.

Darwall, Stephen. (2006). *The Second Person Standpoint: Morality, Respect, and Accountability.* Harvard University Press

Darwall, Stephen, Gibbard, Allan, and Railton, Peter. (1992). Toward *fin de siecle* Ethics: Some Trends. *The Philosophical Review*, **101:** 115–89. Reprinted in Stephen Darwall, Allan Gibbard, and Peter Railton, eds. (1997). *Moral Discourse and Practice.* New York: Oxford University Press, pp. 3–47.

Dorsey, Dale. (2018). A Perfectionist Humean Constructivism. *Ethics*, **128(3):** 574–602.

Driver, Julia. (2017). Contingency and Constructivism. In Simon Kirchin, ed., *Reading Parfit.* London: Routledge, pp. 172–88.

Engstrom, Stephen. (2009). *The Form of Practical Knowledge.* Cambridge: Cambridge University Press.

Engstrom, Stephen. (2013). Constructivism and Practical Knowledge. In Bagnoli 2013, pp. 133–52.

Enoch, David. (2006). Agency, Shmagency: Why Normativity Won't Come from What Is Constitutive of Agency. *Philosophical Review*, **115:** 169–98.

Enoch, David. (2009). Can There Be a Global, Interesting, Coherent Constructivism About Practical Reason? *Philosophical Explorations*, **12:** 319–39.

Enoch, David. (2011). Shmagency revisited. In Michael Brady (ed.), *New Waves in Metaethics.* Palgrave-Macmillan

Ferrero, Luca. (2009). Constitutivism and the Inescapability of Agency. *Oxford Studies in Metaethics*, **4:** 303–33.

Ferrero, Luca. (2019). The Simple Constitutivist Move. *Philosophical Explorations*, **22(2):** 146–62.

Fitzpatrick, William J. (2005). The Practical Turn in Ethical Theory: Korsgaard's Constructivism, Realism and the Nature of Normativity. *Ethics*, **115:** 651–91.

FitzPatrick, William J. (2013). How Not to Be an Ethical Constructivist: A Critique of Korsgaard's Neo-Kantian Constitutivism. In Bagnoli 2013, pp. 41–62.

Fix, Jeremy David. (2020). The Error Condition. *Canadian Journal of Philosophy*, **50(1):** 34–48.

Fix, Jeremy David. (2021). Two Sorts of Constitutivism. *Analytic Philosophy*, **62(1):** 1–20.

Foot, Philippa. (1972). Morality as a system of hypothetical imperatives. *Philosophical Review*, **81 (3):305-316.**

Frankfurt, Harry G. (2004). *Reasons of Love*. NJ: Princeton University Press.

Frankfurt, Harry G. (2006). *Taking Ourselves Seriously and Getting It Right*. Stanford: Stanford University Press.

Galvin, Richard. (2011). Rounding Up the Usual Suspects: Varieties of Kantian Constructivism in Ethics. *The Philosophical Quarterly*, **61(242):** 16–36.

Gaut, Berys. (1997). The Structure of Practical Reason. In Garrett Cullity and Berys Gaut, eds., *Ethics and Practical Reason*. Oxford: Clarendon Press, pp. 161–88.

Gauthier, David. (1986). *Morals by Agreement*. Oxford: Oxford University Press.

Gibbard, Allan. (1990). *Wise Choices, Apt Feelings: A Theory of Normative Judgement*. Cambridge, MA: Harvard University Press.

Gibbard, Allan. (1999). Morality as Consistency in Living. *Ethics*, **110:** 140–64.

Gledhill, James and Sebastian Stein, eds. (2020). *Hegel and Contemporary Practical Philosophy: Beyond Kantian Constructivism*. London: Routledge.

Gobsch, Wolfram. (2019). Autonomy and Radical Evil: A Kantian Challenge to Constitutivism. *Philosophical Explorations*, **22(2):** 194–207.

Gowans, Christopher W. (2002). Practical Identities and Autonomy: Korsgaard's Reformation of Kant's Moral Philosophy. *Philosophy and Phenomenological Research*, **64(3):** 546–70.

Guyer, Paul. (2013). Constructivism and Self-Constitution. In Mark Timmons and Sorin Baiasu, eds., *Kant on Practical Justification: Interpretive Essays*. Oxford: Oxford University Press, pp. 176–200.

Guyer, Paul. (2017) *The Virtues of Freedom*, Oxford University Press.

Harman, Gilbert. (1997). Practical Reasoning. In Alfred Mele, ed., *The Philosophy of Action*. Oxford: Oxford University Press, pp. 149–77.

Hegel, F. G. (1991). *Elements of the Philosophy of Right*. Cambridge: Cambridge University Press.

Herman, Barbara. (2008). *Moral Literacy*. Cambridge, MA: Harvard University Press.

Herman, Barbara. (2000). Editor's Forward, in John Rawls, *Lectures on the History of Moral Philosophy*. Harvard University Press, pp. x-xix.

Hill, Thomas Jr. E. (1989). Kantian Constructivism in Ethics. *Ethics*, **99**: 752–70.

Hill, Thomas Jr. E. (1994). *Respect for Humanity. Tanner Lectures on Human Values*. CA: Stanford University Press.

Hill, Thomas Jr. E. (2001). Hypothetical Consent in Kantian Constructivism. *Social Philosophy and Policy*, **18**: 300–29. Reprinted in Hill, Thomas. Jr. E. (2002). *Human Welfare and Moral Worth: Kantian Perspectives*. Oxford University Press, pp. 61–95.

Hill, Thomas Jr. E. (2008). Moral Construction as a Task: Sources and Limits. *Social Philosophy and Policy*, **25(1)**: 214–36. Reprinted in Ellen Frankel Paul, Fred D. Miller, and Paul Jeffrey, eds. (2008). *Objectivity, Subjectivism, and Relativism in Ethics*. Cambridge: Cambridge University Press.

Hume, David. (1985). Of the Standard of Taste. In Eugene F. Miller, ed., *Essays: Moral, Political, and Literary*. Indianapolis: Liberty Fund, pp. 226–49.

Hume, David. (2007). *A Treatise of Human Nature*. Oxford: Oxford University Press.

Hursthouse, Rosalind. (1987). *Beginning Lives*. Oxford: Blackwell.

Hussain, Nadeem and Shah, Nishi. (2006). Misunderstanding Metaethics: Korsgaard's Rejection of Realism. *Oxford Studies in Metaethics*, **1**: 265–94.

James, Aaron. (2007). Constructivism About Practical Reasons. *Philosophy and Phenomenological Research*, **74(2)**: 302–25.

James, Aaron. (2012). Constructing Protagorean Objectivity. In Lenman and Shemmer 2012, pp. 60–80.

Kant, Immanuel. (1781). *Critique of Pure Reason, Grundlegung zur Metaphysik der Sitten, Kants gesammelte Schriften*, Preussische Akademie der Wissenschaften, Berlin, Paul Guyer and Allen W. Wood (1998). Cambridge: Cambridge University Press [C1].

Kant, Immanuel. (1785). *Grundlegung zur Metaphysik der Sitten, Kants gesammelte Schriften*, Preussische Akademie der Wissenschaften, Berlin, Volume 4, *Groundwork of the Metaphysic of Morals*. In Allen W. Wood, ed. (1983). *Practical Philosophy*. Cambridge: Cambridge University Press [Abbreviated G].

Kant, Immanuel. (1786). *What Does It Mean to Orient Oneself in Thinking?* In Allen W. Wood and G. di Giovanni, trans. (1996). *Religion and Rational Theology*. Cambridge University Press, **8: 133–46** [Abbreviated WOT].

Kant, Immanuel. (1788). *Critique of Practical Reason, Kants gesammelte Schriften*, Preussische Akademie der Wissenschaften, Berlin, 1907, Volume 5. In Allen W. Wood, ed. (1983). *Practical Philosophy*. Cambridge: Cambridge University Press [Abbreviated C2].

Kant, Immanuel. (1797). *Metaphysics of Morals, Kants gesammelte Schriften*, Preussische Akademie der Wissenschaften, Berlin, 1907, Volume 6. In Mary J. Gregorm ed. (1996). Practical Philosophy. Cambridge: Cambridge University Press [Abbreviated MM].

Katsafanas, Paul. (2018). Constitutivism About Practical Reasons. In Daniel Star, ed., *The Oxford Handbook of Reasons and Normativity*. Oxford: Oxford University Press, pp. 367–94.

Kleingeld, Pauline. (1999). Kant, History, and the Idea of Moral Development. *History of Philosophy Quarterly*, **16(1)**: 59–80.

Kleingeld, Pauline. (2010). Moral Consciousness and the "Fact of Reason." In Andrews Reath and Jens Timmermann, eds., *Kant's Critique of Practical Reason: A Critical Guide*. Cambridge: Cambridge University Press, pp. 55–72.

Korsgaard, Christine M. (1989). Personal Identity and the Unity of Agency: A Kantian Response to Parfit. *Philosophy and Public Affairs*, **18(2)**: 103–31.

Korsgaard, Christine M. (1996a). *Sources of Normativity*. Cambridge: Cambridge University Press.

Korsgaard, Christine M. (1996b). *Creating the Kingdom of Ends*. Cambridge: Cambridge University Press.

Korsgaard, Christine M. (1997). The Normativity of Instrumental Reason. In G. Cullity and B. Gaut eds., *Ethics and Practical Reason*. Oxford: Clarendon Press. Reprinted in Korsgaard 2008, pp. 27–68.

Korsgaard, Christine M. (1998). Motivation, Metaphysics, and the Value of Self. *Ethics*, **109**: 49–66.

Korsgaard, Christine M. (2003). Realism and Constructivism in Twentieth-Century Moral Philosophy. *The Journal of Philosophical Research, APA Centennial Supplement, Philosophy in America at the End of the Century*, **2003**: 99–122.

Korsgaard, Christine M. (2008). *The Constitution of Agency*. Oxford: Oxford University Press.

Korsgaard, Christine M. (2008). The General Point of View: Love and Moral Approval in Hume's Ethics. In Korsgaard 2009, pp.263–301.

Korsgaard, Christine M. (2009). *Self-Constitution: Action, Identity and Integrity*. Oxford University Press.

Korsgaard, Christine M. (2011). Natural Goodness, Rightness, and the Intersubjectivity of Reason: Reply to Arroyo, Cummiskey, Moland, and Bird-Pollan. *Metaphilosophy*, **42(4)**: 381–94.

Korsgaard, Christine M. (2019). Constitutivism and the Virtues. *Philosophical Explorations*, **22(2)**: 98–116.

Krasnoff, Larry. (1999). How Kantian Is Constructivism? *Kant-Studien*, **90 (90):** 385–409.

Laitinen, Arto. (2020). Finding by Making: The Mediating Role of Social Constructions, Commitments, and Resonance in Hegelian Normative Realism. In Gledhill and Stein 2020, chapter 8.

Lavin, Douglas. (2004). Practical Reason and the Possibility of Error. *Ethics*, **114:** 424–57.

LeBar, Mark. (2005). Eudaimonist Autonomy. *American Philosophical Quarterly*, **42(3)**: 171–83.

Lebar, Mark. (2008). Aristotelian Constructivism. *Social Philosophy and Policy*, **25(1):** 182–213.

Lebar, Mark. (2013). Constructivism and Particularism. In Bagnoli 2013, pp. 183–200.

Leffler, Olof. (2019). New Shmagency Worries. *Journal of Ethics and Social Philosophy*, **15(2):** 121–45.

Lenman, James. (1998). Review of Korsgaard's *Creating the Kingdom of Ends*. *Ethical Theory and Moral Practice* 1 (4):487-8.

Lenman, James. (2010). "Humean Constructivism in Moral Theory", *Oxford Studies in Metaethics*, 5: 175–193.

Lenman, James. (2012). "Expressivism and Contructivism". In Lenman & Shemmer 2012: 213–25.

Lenman, James and Shemmer, Yonatan. (2012). *Constructivism in Practical Philosophy*. Oxford University Press.

Mackie, J. L. (1977). *Ethics: Inventing Right and Wrong*. London: Penguin.

McDowell, John. (1979). Virtue and Reason. *The Monist*, **62(3):** 331–50.

McDowell, John. (1981). Non-Cognitivism and Rule-Following. In Steven Holtzman and Christopher Leich, eds., *Wittgenstein: To Follow a Rule*. London: Routledge & Kegan Paul.

McDowell, John. (1995). Two Sorts of Naturalism. In Rosalind Hursthouse, Gawin Lawrence and Warren Quinn, eds., *Virtues and Reasons*. Oxford: Clarendon Press.

Mitchell-Yellin, Benjamin. (2015). Aligning with the Good. *Journal of Ethics and Social Philosophy*, **9(2):** 1–8.

Moland, Lydia. (2011). Agency and Practical Identity: A Hegelian Response to Korsgaard. *Metaphilosophy*, **42(4):** 368–75.

Moyar, Dean. (2011). *Hegel's Conscience*. New York: Oxford University Press.

Nagel, Thomas. (1996). Universality and the reflective self. In C. Korsgaard, *The Sources of Normativity*. Cambridge: Cambridge University Press, pp. 200-209.

Ng, Karen. (2009). Hegel's Logic of Actuality. *The Review of Metaphysics,* **63** (**1**): 139–72.

O'Neill, Onora. (1975). *Acting on Principle.* NY: Columbia University Press.

O'Neill, Onora. (1989). *Constructions of Reason.* Cambridge: Cambridge University Press.

O'Neill, Onora. (1996). *Toward Justice and Virtue: A Constructivist Account of Practical Reasoning.* Cambridge: Cambridge University Press.

O'Neill, Onora. (1999). "Kantian Constructivisms", in *Rationalität, Realismus, Revision. Vorträge des 3. internationalen Kongresses der Gesellschaft für Analytische Philosophie vom 15. bis zum 18. September 1997 in München,* Julian Nida-Rümelin, ed., Berlin, New York: De Gruyter, pp. 3–16. doi:10.1515/9783110805703.3

O'Neill, Onora. (2003). Constructivism in Rawls and Kant. In Samuel. Freeman, ed., *The Cambridge Companion to Rawls.* Cambridge: Cambridge University Press, pp. 347–67.

O'Neill, Onora. (2015). *Constructing Authorities.* Cambridge: Cambridge University Press.

O'Shea, James. (2006). Conceptual Connections: Kant and the Twentieth-Century Analytic Tradition. In Graham. Bird, ed., *Companion to Kant.* Oxford: Blackwell, pp. 513–26.

Ostritsch, Sebastian. (2020). Hegel's Metaethical Non-Constructivism. In Gledhill and Stein 2020, chapter 4.

Parfit, Derek. (2011). *On What Matters.* Oxford: Oxford University Press.

Pippin, Robert B. (2008). *Hegel's Practical Philosophy – Rational Agency as Ethical Life.* Cambridge: Cambridge University Press.

Pollok, Konstantin. (2017). Kant's Farewell to Perfectionism. In Pollok, *Kant's Theory of Normativity: Exploring the Space of Reason.* Cambridge: Cambridge University Press, pp. 27–57.

Putnam, Hilary. (1981). *Realism, Truth and History.* Cambridge: Cambridge University Press.

Putnam, Hilary. (1990). *Realism with Human Face.* Cambridge, MA: Harvard University Press.

Rawls, John. (1951). Outline of a Decision Procedure for Ethics. *Philosophical Review,* **60**(2): 177–97. Reprinted in Samuel. Freeman, ed. (1999). *Collected Papers.* Cambridge: Cambridge University Press, pp. 1–19.

Rawls, John (1955). Two Concepts of Rules. *Philosophical Review* **64 (1):3-32.**

Rawls, John. (1980). Kantian Constructivism in Moral Theory. *Journal of Philosophy,* **77**: 515–72. Reprinted in Samuel. Freeman, ed. (1999). *Collected Papers.* Cambridge: Cambridge University Press, pp. 303–58.

Rawls, John. (1989). Themes in Kant's Moral Philosophy. Reprinted in Samuel. Freeman, ed. (1999). *Collected Papers*. Cambridge: Cambridge University Press, pp. 497–528.

Rawls, John. (1993). *Political Liberalism*. New York: Columbia University Press.

Rawls, John. (2000). *Lectures on the History of Moral Philosophy*. Edited by Barbara Herman, Cambridge, MA: Harvard University Press.

Reath, Andrews. (2006). *Agency and Autonomy in Kant's Moral Theory*. Oxford: Clarendon Press.

Redding, Paul. (2020). Hegel's "Actualist" Idealism and the Modality of Practical Reason. In Gledhill and Stein 2020, chapter 1.

Richardson, Henry. (2013). Revising Moral Norms: Pragmatism and the Problem of Perspicuous Description. In Bagnoli 2013, pp. 221–42.

Richardson, Henry. (2018). *Articulating the Moral Community*. New York: Oxford University Press.

Ridge, Michael. (2012). Kantian constructivism: something old, something new. In James Lenman & Yonatan Shemmer eds., *Constructivism in Practical Philosophy*. Oxford University Press.

Rosati, Connie S. (2003). Agency and the open question argument. *Ethics* **113** (3):490-527.

Rosati, Connie S. (2016). Agents and "Shmagents": An Essay on Agency and Normativity. *Oxford Studies in Metaethics* **11**: 182–213.

Ronzoni, Miriam. (2010). Constructivism and Practical Reason: On Intersubjectivity, Abstraction, and Judgement. *The Journal of Moral Philosophy*, **4:** 74–104.

Saemi, Amir. (2016). The Form of Practical Knowledge and Implicit Cognition: A Critique of Kantian Constitutivism. *Social Theory and Practice*, **42(4):** 733–47.

Scanlon, Thomas M. (1998). *What We Owe to Each Other*. Cambridge, MA: Bellknap Press.

Scanlon, Thomas M. (2002). Rawls on Justification. In Samuel. Freeman, ed., *The Cambridge Companion to Rawls*. Cambridge: Cambridge University Press, pp. 139–67.

Scanlon, Thomas M. (2003). Metaphysics and Morals. *Proceedings and Addresses of the American Philosophical Association*, **77(2):** 7–22.

Scanlon, Thomas M. (2007). Structural Irrationality. In Geoffrey Brennan, Robert E. Goodin, Frank Jackson, and Michael Smith, eds., *Common Minds: Themes from the Philosophy of Philip Pettit*. New York: Oxford University Press, pp. 84–103.

Scanlon, Thomas M. (2012). "The Appeal and Limits of Constructivism", in Lenman and Shemmer 2012a: 226–42.

Scanlon, Thomas M. (2014). *Being Realistic About Reasons*. New York: Oxford University Press.

Schafer, Karl. (forthcoming). Practical Cognition and Knowledge of Things-in-Themselves. In Evan Tiffany and Dai Heide, eds., *Kantian Freedom*. New York: Oxford University Press.

Schafer, Karl. (2014). Constructivism and Three Forms of Perspective-Dependence in Metaethics. *Philosophy and Phenomenological Research*, **89(1):** 68–101.

Schafer, Karl. (2015a). Realism and Constructivism in Kantian Metaethics 1: Realism and Constructivism in a Kantian Context. *Philosophy Compass*, **10:** 690–701.

Schafer, Karl. (2015b). Realism and Constructivism in Kantian Metaethics 2: The Kantian Conception of Rationality and Rationalist Constructivism. *Philosophy Compass*, **10**: 702–13.

Schafer, Karl. (2018). A Kantian Virtue Epistemology: Rational Capacities and Transcendental Arguments. *Synthese*, **198(Suppl 13):** 3113–36.

Schafer, Karl. (2019a). Kant: Constitutivism as Capacities-First Philosophy. *Philosophical Explorations*, **22(2):** 177–93.

Schafer, Karl. (2019b). The Artificial Virtues of Thought: Hume on the Normativity of Cognition. *Philosopher's Imprint*, **19/7**.

Schroeder, Mark. (2007). *Slaves of the Passions*. New York: Oxford University Press.

Shafer-Landau, Russ. (2003). *Moral Realism*. Oxford: Clarendon Press.

Skorupski, John. (1998). Rescuing moral obligation. *European Journal of Philosophy* **6 (3):** 335–355.

Skorupski, John. (2010). *The Domain of Reason*. Oxford: Oxford University Press.

Smith, Michael. (1994). *The Moral Problem*. Oxford: Oxford University Press.

Smith, Michael. (1999). Search for the Source. *The Philosophical Quarterly*, **49:** 384–94.

Smith, Michael. (2013). A Constitutivist Theory of Reasons: Its Promise and Parts. *Law, Ethics and Philosophy*, **1:** 9–30.

Smith, Michael. (2015). The Magic of Constitutivism. *American Philosophical Quarterly*, **52(2):** 187–200.

Southwood, Nicholas. (2008). Vindicating the Normativity of Rationality. *Ethics*, **119:** 9–30.

Southwood, Nicholas. (2018). Constructivism About Reason. In Daniel Star, ed., *The Oxford Handbook of Reasons and Normativity*. Oxford: Oxford University Press, pp. 342–66.

Stein, Sebastian. (2020). Choosing to Do the Right Thing: Aristotle, Kant, and Hegel on Practical Normativity and the Realism-Constructivism Debate. In Gledhill and Stein 2020, chapter 2.

Stern, Robert. (2000). *Transcendental Arguments: Answering the Question of Justification*. Oxford: Oxford University Press, pp. 75-94.

Stern, Robert. (2011). The Value of Humanity: Reflections on Korsgaard's Transcendental Argument. In J. Smith and P. Sullivan, eds., *Transcendental Philosophy and Naturalism*. Oxford: Oxford University Press, pp. 74–95.

Stern, Robert. (2012). *Understanding Moral Obligation: Kant, Hegel, Kierkegaard*. Cambridge University Press.

Stern, Robert. (2013). Moral Skepticism, Constructivism and the Value of Humanity. In Bagnoli 2013, pp. 22–40.

Stevenson, Charles Leslie. (1937). The emotive meaning of ethical terms. *Mind* **46 (181):**14-31.

Street, Sharon. (2006). A Darwinian Dilemma for Realist Theories of Value. *Philosophical Studies*, **127(1):** 109−66.

Street, Sharon. (2008a). Constructivism About Reasons. *Oxford Studies in Metaethics*, **3:** 207–45.

Street, Sharon. (2008b). Reply to Copp: Naturalism, Normativity, and the Varieties of Realism Worth Worrying About. *Philosophical Issues*, **18(1):** 207–28.

Street, Sharon. (2009). In Defense of Future Tuesday' Indifference: Ideally Coherent Eccentrics and the Contingency of What Matters. *Philosophical Issues*, **19(1):** 273–98.

Street, Sharon. (2010). What is Constructivism in Ethics and Metaethics? *Philosophy Compass*, **5:** 363–84.

Street, Sharon. (2011). Mind-Independence without the Mystery: Why Quasi-Realists Can't Have It Both Ways. In Russ Shafer-Landau, ed., *Oxford Studies in Metaethics, Volume 6*. Oxford: Oxford University Press, pp. 1–32.

Street, Sharon. (2012). "Coming to Terms with Contingency: Humean Constructivism about Practical Reason", Lenman and Shemmer 2012, pp. 40–59.

Taylor, Jacqueline. (2015). *Reflecting Subjects: Passion, Sympathy, and Society in Hume's Philosophy*. Oxford: Oxford University Press.

Tenenbaum, Sergio. (2019). Formalism and Constitutivism in Kantian Practical Philosophy. *Philosophical Explorations*, **22(2):** 163–76.

Thompson, Michael J. (2004). What is it to Wrong Someone? A Puzzle About Justice. In R. Jay Wallace, Philip Pettit, Samuel Scheffler, and Michael Smith, eds., *Reason and Value: Themes from the Moral Philosophy of Joseph Raz*. Oxford: Clarendon Press, pp. 333–84.

Thompson, Michael J (2008). *Life and Action: Elementary Structures of Practice and Practical Thought.* Cambridge, MA: Harvard University Press.

Thompson, Michael J. (2020). Critical Agency in Hegelian Ethics: Social Metaphysics versus Moral Constructivism. In Gledhill and Stein 2020, chapter 10.

Tiffany, Evan. (2006). How Kantian Must Kantian Constructivists Be? *Inquiry,* **49:** 524–46.

Timmons, Mark. (2003). The Limits of Moral Constructivism. *Ratio,* **16(4):** 391–423.

Timmons, Mark ed. (2015). *Reason, Value, and Respect: Kantian Themes from the Philosophy of Thomas E. Hill, Jr.* Oxford: Oxford University Press.

Timmons, Mark. (2017). *Significance and System: Essays on Kant's Ethics.* Oxford: Oxford University Press.

Tropman, Elizabeth (2014). Evolutionary debunking arguments: moral realism, constructivism, and explaining moral knowledge. *Philosophical Explorations* **17 (2):**126-140.

Tubert, Ariela (2010). Constitutive arguments. *Philosophy Compass* **5 (8):**656-666.

Vavova, Katia. (2014). Debunking Evolutionary Debunking. In Russ Shafer-Landau, ed., *Oxford Studies in Metaethics,* **9:** 76–101.

Velleman, J. David. (2004). Review: Replies to Discussion on "The Possibility of Practical Reason". *Philosophical Studies* **121 (3):**277–298.

Velleman, J. David. (2009). *How We Get Along.* Cambridge: Cambridge University Press.

Walden, Kenneth. (2012). Laws of Nature, Laws of Freedom, and the Social Construction of Normativity. In Russ Shafer-Landau, ed., *Oxford Studies in Metaethics,* **7:** 37–79.

Walden, Kenneth. (2018). Practical Reason Not as Such. *Journal of Ethics and Social Philosophy,* **2:** 127–52.

Wallace, R. Jay. (2019). *The Moral Nexus.* NJ: Princeton University Press.

Watkins, Eric (2019). *Kant on Laws.* Cambridge: Cambridge University Press.

Watkins, Eric and Fitzpatrick, William. (2002). O'Neill and Korsgaard on the Construction of Normativity. *Journal of Value Inquiry,* **36:** 349–67.

Way, Jonathan. (2010). The Normativity of Rationality. *Philosophy Compass,* **5:** 1057–68.

Westphal, Kenneth R. (2016). *How Hume and Kant Reconstruct Natural Law: Justifying Strict Objectivity without Debating Moral Realism.* Oxford: Oxford University Press.

Westphal, Kenneth R. (2017). Hegel's Natural Law Constructivism: Progress in Principle and in Practice. In T. Brooks and S. Stein, eds., *Hegel's Political Philosophy: On the Normative Significance of Method and System*. Oxford: Oxford University Press, pp. 253–79.

Williams, Bernard A.O. (1981). *Moral Luck*. Cambridge: Cambridge University Press.

Williams, Bernard A.O. (1985). *Ethics and the Limits of Philosophy*, Cambridge, MA: Harvard University Press.

Williams, Bernard A.O. (1993). *Shame and Necessity*. Cambridge: Cambridge University Press.

Williams, Bernard A.O. (1996). History, Morality, and the Test of Reflection. In Christine M. Korsgaard and Onora O'Neill, eds., *The Sources of Normativity*. Cambridge: Cambridge University Press, pp. 210–18.

Wong, David. (2008). Constructing Normative Objectivity in Ethics. *Social Philosophy and Policy*, **25(1)**: 237–66.

Wood, Allen W. (1995). Attacking Morality: A Metaethical Project. *Canadian Journal of Philosophy*, **25**: 221–49.

Wood, Allen W. (1999). *Kant's Ethical Thought*, Cambridge: Cambridge University Press.

Wood, Allen W. (2017). How a Kantian Decides What to Do. In Matthew Altman, ed., *The Palgrave Kant Handbook/Palgrave Handbooks in German Idealism*. London: Palgrave Macmillan, pp. 263–84.

Wretzel, Joshua I. (2020). Constraint and the Ethical Agent: Hegel Between Constructivism and Realism. In Gledhill and Stein 2020, chapter 3.

Yeomans, Christopher. (2012). *Freedom and Reflection: Hegel and the Logic of Agency*. Oxford: Oxford University Press.

Yeomans, Christopher. (2020). Historical Constructivism. In Gledhill and Stein 2020, chapter 9.

Cambridge Elements ≡

Ethics

Ben Eggleston
University of Kansas

Ben Eggleston is a professor of philosophy at the University of Kansas. He is the editor of John Stuart Mill, *Utilitarianism: With Related Remarks from Mill's Other Writings* (Hackett, 2017) and a co-editor of *Moral Theory and Climate Change: Ethical Perspectives on a Warming Planet* (Routledge, 2020), *The Cambridge Companion to Utilitarianism* (Cambridge, 2014), and *John Stuart Mill and the Art of Life* (Oxford, 2011). He is also the author of numerous articles and book chapters on various topics in ethics.

Dale E. Miller
Old Dominion University, Virginia

Dale E. Miller is a professor of philosophy at Old Dominion University. He is the author of *John Stuart Mill: Moral, Social and Political Thought* (Polity, 2010) and a co-editor of *Moral Theory and Climate Change: Ethical Perspectives on a Warming Planet* (Routledge, 2020), *A Companion to Mill* (Blackwell, 2017), *The Cambridge Companion to Utilitarianism* (Cambridge, 2014), *John Stuart Mill and the Art of Life* (Oxford, 2011), and *Morality, Rules, and Consequences: A Critical Reader* (Edinburgh, 2000). He is also the editor-in-chief of *Utilitas*, and the author of numerous articles and book chapters on various topics in ethics broadly construed.

About the Series
This Elements series provides an extensive overview of major figures, theories, and concepts in the field of ethics. Each entry in the series acquaints students with the main aspects of its topic while articulating the author's distinctive viewpoint in a manner that will interest researchers.

Cambridge Elements ⁼

Ethics

Elements in the Series

A full series listing is available at www.cambridge.org/EETH

Printed in the United States
by Baker & Taylor Publisher Services